DK EYEWITNESS
PRESIDENTS

Written by
JAMES G. BARBER

In Association with the

Smithsonian

Fan commemorating Lincoln

Theodore Roosevelt banner

Carter campaign memorabilia

Anti-Nixon buttons

McKinley campaign umbrella

Penguin Random House

CREATED BY LEAPFROG PRESS LTD.
Senior Editor and Co-Author Bridget Hopkinson
Editor Jacky Jackson   Art Director Miranda Kennedy
Art Editors Catherine Goldsmith and Adrienne Hutchinson
Picture Researcher Liz Moore

DK PUBLISHING
Publisher Neal Porter   Executive Editor Iris Rosoff   Art Director Dirk Kaufman

SECOND EDITION
Project Editor Elizabeth Hester   Designer Miesha Tate
Assistant Managing Art Editor Michelle Baxter   Publisher Chuck Lang
Creative Director Tina Vaughan   Production Chris Avgherinos

THIRD EDITION
Editor John Searcy   Additional Text Amy Pastan   Publishing Director Beth Sutinis
Designers Jessica Park, Bill Miller, Danielle Delaney   Jacket Designer Andrew Smith
CD Designer Sunita Gahir   Managing Art Editor Michelle Baxter

FOURTH EDITION
Senior Editor Rebecca Warren   Editorial Director Nancy Ellwood
Designer Jessica Park

RELAUNCH EDITION
DK US
Senior Editor Margaret Parrish   Additional Text Margaret Parrish
Editorial Director Nancy Ellwood

DK INDIA
Assistant Art Editor Nidhi Rastogi   DTP Designer Pawan Kumar
Senior DTP Designer Harish Aggarwal
Picture Researcher Sakshi Saluja   Jacket Designer Surabhi Wadhwa
Managing Editor Kingshuk Ghoshal   Managing Art Editor Govind Mittal

DK UK
Senior Art Editor Spencer Holbrook   Jacket Editor Claire Gell
Jacket Design Development Manager Sophia MTT
Producer, pre-production Jacqueline Street   Producer Vivienne Yong
Managing Editor Francesca Baines   Managing Art Editor Philip Letsu
Publisher Andrew Macintyre   Associate Publishing Director Liz Wheeler
Art Director Karen Self   Design Director Phil Ormerod
Publishing Director Jonathan Metcalf

First American Edition, 2000
This edition published in the United States in 2017 by
DK Publishing, 345 Hudson Street, New York, New York 10014

A WORLD OF IDEAS:
SEE ALL THERE IS TO KNOW

www.dk.com

Carter bumper stickers

Eyeglasses belonging to James K. Polk

Life magazine cover from the Coolidge era

Lewis and Clark compass from Jefferson's presidency

Teddy bear named after Teddy Roosevelt

Contents

Buchanan campaign flag

George Washington's field kit from the Revolutionary War

George Washington

Compass belonging to Washington

In 1789, George Washington became the first president of the United States of America. The American colonies had won independence from Great Britain in the Revolutionary War. Washington was a war hero and the first choice for president. He was "a wise, a good, and a great man," stated Thomas Jefferson, and he showed wisdom in launching the new government. His example has defined the presidency ever since.

This is the military mess kit that George Washington carried with him in the Revolutionary War.

General Washington leads his troops across the Delaware River on Christmas Day, 1776.

Revolutionary leadership

As a young man, Washington became commander of the colonial army in Virginia and fought against the French and the Indians. When the Revolutionary War began in 1775, he was chosen to lead American forces. Although not a great strategist, he had determination and succeeded in holding his badly equipped army together and securing victory in 1781.

Crossing the Delaware River

Defeated at Long Island in August, the Patriot cause seemed lost by December 1776, until Washington struck back. On December 25, he led his 2,400-man army across the river at night. Surprising the enemy, he won a victory at Trenton, New Jersey.

Patriot medal celebrating an early victory over the British at Boston, March 1776

During the war, Washington would have spent long hours in this camp tent planning his next move against the British

Forging the Constitution

In 1787, Washington presided over the Constitutional Convention in Philadelphia and helped draft a new system of democratic government. It had three branches, each of which was intended to exercise checks and balances over the others. The Senate and the House of Representatives would make the laws in the legislative branch, the Supreme Court would dispense justice in the judiciary branch, and the president would enforce the laws in the executive branch. In addition to the central government, state and local governments would comprise the American system of democracy.

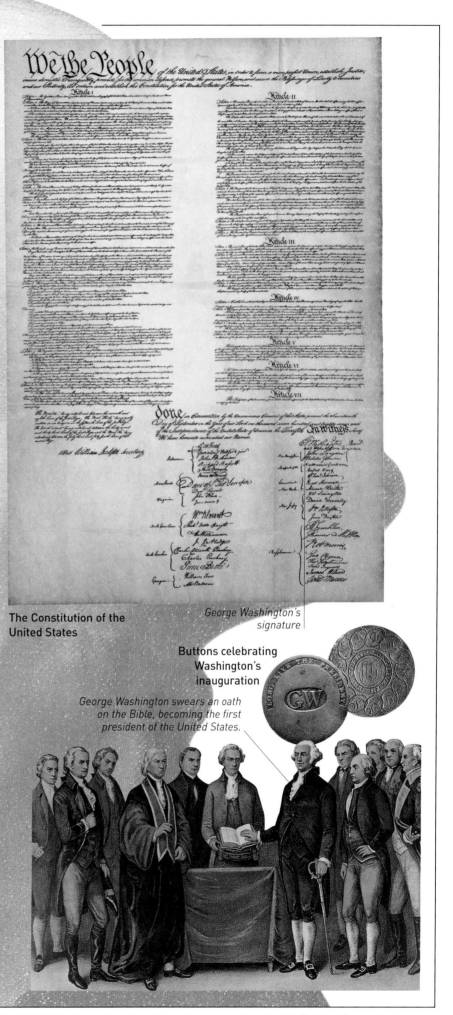

The Constitution of the United States

George Washington's signature

Buttons celebrating Washington's inauguration

George Washington swears an oath on the Bible, becoming the first president of the United States.

The new president

George Washington's powers as president were set out clearly under the new Constitution. It was his responsibility to make sure that the laws of the land were followed and to appoint high-ranking government officials and judges. He also had the power to command the armed forces and to make treaties with other countries. Washington was so admired by the people that he probably could have been president for as long as he wished. But the Constitution stated that each president should serve a four-year term of office and then stand for reelection. Washington did this, and after two terms, he decided that he had served long enough.

Continued on next page

Washington at home

George Washington grew up on a farm near the Rappahannock River in Virginia. At age 20, he inherited the Mount Vernon estate and became one of the largest landowners in northern Virginia. He considered farming "the most noble employment of man." When at home, he filled his days with the running of his plantation and pursued sports such as hunting and fishing. Much of his time in his later years was spent with his wife, Martha, entertaining the many guests who visited Mount Vernon every year.

Washington's set of false teeth

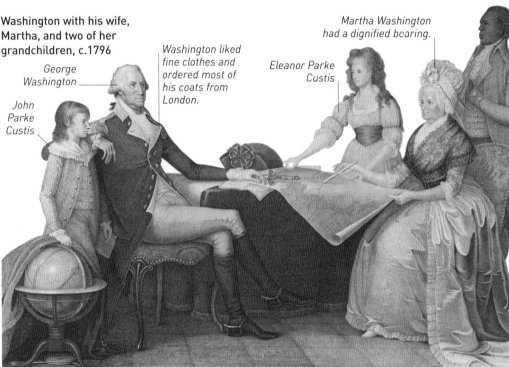

Washington with his wife, Martha, and two of her grandchildren, c.1796

George Washington

John Parke Custis

Washington liked fine clothes and ordered most of his coats from London.

Eleanor Parke Custis

Martha Washington had a dignified bearing.

Mount Vernon

In his years at Mount Vernon, Washington improved the house and added land to his estate, until it covered more than 8,000 acres (3,240 Ha). He experimented with new scientific ways of improving his crops and livestock, and he especially enjoyed planting trees, several of which still tower over the estate today.

Martha Washington

In January 1759, George Washington married a wealthy widow, Martha Dandridge Custis. Although the couple remained childless, Washington became father to Martha's two children from her first marriage. When Washington was elected president, Martha grew into her role of first lady, hosting official receptions with great decorum.

The Whiskey Rebellion

In 1794, Washington's authority as president was tested for the first time when a rebellion broke out in Pennsylvania. Farmers were angry about a new federal whiskey tax. The governor of Pennsylvania refused to enforce the tax, so Washington sent an army to ensure that the law was obeyed. His swift, decisive action sent a clear message.

A federal officer tarred and feathered by angry farmers

Presidential entertaining

George Washington believed that as president he should behave with reserve and dignity. He was formal with colleagues and traveled in a splendid horsedrawn carriage. Dinners were formal; guests referred to their hosts as President and Lady Washington.

Indian wars

Conflict between white settlers and Native Americans was a pressing issue for Washington. When US troops were ambushed by Indians of the Northwest Confederation, he sent reinforcments, resulting in a US victory at the Battle of Fallen Timbers. The Confederation lost Ohio in the Treaty of Fort Greenville, 1795.

Seneca chief

Whenever possible, Washington negotiated with tribal chiefs. In 1792, he met the Seneca chief Red Jacket, who agreed to grant land concessions to the US. Washington gave him a silver medal as a sign of good faith.

US officers at the Battle of Fallen Timbers, 1794

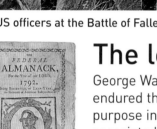

The legend of Washington

George Washington became a legend in his lifetime. He had endured the trials of war and had shown great courage and purpose in helping to forge a nation. His virtues became associated with the character of the new republic. Known as the "Father of His Country," Washington's image appeared on everything, from porcelain to money.

This early likeness of Washington appeared in print in 1792.

Childhood myth

In *Life of Washington* (1806), the author described an early event that showed the leader's honesty. A young Washington reputedly cut down his father's cherry tree. When asked if he did, he said: "I cannot tell a lie. I did it."

Handkerchief with a map of Washington, D.C.

The nation's capital

In 1791, George Washington helped select a site on the Potomac River to be the nation's capital. In his honor, the city was named Washington.

George Washington on a banknote, 1800

George Washington

1ST PRESIDENT
1789–1797

BORN
February 22, 1732
Westmoreland County, Virginia

INAUGURATED AS PRESIDENT
First term: April 30, 1789
Second term: March 4, 1793

AGE AT INAUGURATION
57

PARTY
Federalist

FIRST LADY
Martha Dandridge Custis

CHILDREN ADOPTED BY MARRIAGE
John Parke Custis
Martha Parke Custis

DIED
December 14, 1799
Mount Vernon, Virginia

KEY EVENTS OF PRESIDENCY

1789 Washington appoints Thomas Jefferson as secretary of state and Alexander Hamilton as secretary of the treasury; John Adams is vice president.

1791 A national bank is established; the site for the nation's new capital, Washington, D.C., is selected; the first 10 amendments of the Constitution are ratified.

1792 Congress establishes a national mint.

1793 Washington issues the Proclamation of Neutrality in an attempt to avoid conflict with Great Britain and France, who are at war.

1794 Washington signs the unpopular Jay Treaty with Great Britain, allowing US ships to be inspected at sea in return for the removal of British troops from the Northwest Territory; Washington puts down the Whiskey Rebellion.

John Adams

John Adams was not a popular hero like George Washington. He could be pompous and had many political enemies. Yet he was a Founding Father of the country and helped draft the Declaration of Independence. He also negotiated the treaty that ended the Revolution in 1783. He felt overlooked as Washington's vice president, claiming the role was "the most insignificant office that ever the invention of man contrived." But his loyalty was rewarded. In 1797, Adams became the president. Foreign affairs dominated his term of office.

John Adams was short and stout and had a proud personality.

Cookbook used in the Adams family, c. 1780

His Rotundity

John Adams was born in Braintree, Massachusetts, and studied law at Harvard University. By his own admission, he was "puffy, vain, conceited," and as George Washington's vice president, he encouraged the Senate to bestow grand titles on members of the new government. Adams's detractors referred to him as "His Rotundity."

Father of the Navy

When Adams became president, Great Britain and France were at war. Although the United States was neutral, the French attacked US ships to keep them from trading with Britain, so Adams established a naval department. For two years, French and US frigates engaged in battle at sea. In 1800, Adams negotiated an end to the hostilities.

Abigail Adams

Before he married his wife, Abigail, John Adams sent her a list of her "Faults, Imperfections, (and) Defects." Yet her faults must have been few because she excelled as a politician's wife. While her husband was away, Abigail ran their farm. Under her direction, the family prospered; among her five children, she reared a future president, John Quincy Adams. Their marriage was a happy one and lasted more than 50 years.

Vest belonging to John Adams

Alexander Hamilton

John Adams

2ND PRESIDENT
1797–1801

BORN
October 30, 1735 Braintree
(now Quincy), Massachusetts

INAUGURATED AS PRESIDENT
March 4, 1797

AGE AT INAUGURATION
61

PARTY
Federalist

FIRST LADY
Abigail Smith

CHILDREN
Abigail Amelia
John Quincy
Susanna
Charles
Thomas Boylston

DIED
July 4, 1826
Quincy, Massachusetts

Party politics

In Adams's time, the role of government was hotly debated, and two political parties were formed. The Federalists, led by Alexander Hamilton (above), believed in a strong central government that protected the interests of landowners and industrialists. The Democratic-Republicans, led by Thomas Jefferson, favored the rights of states to decide in matters concerning themselves. Adams was often caught in the middle.

The battleship USS Constitution was first launched in 1797; after restoration, she sailed again in 1997.

BUILDING THE FIRST WHITE HOUSE
WASHINGTON D.C. 1798

Fit for a president

In 1800, Adams and his family moved into the unfinished presidential residence. On his second night, Adams wrote: "I pray Heaven to bestow the best Blessings on this House and all that shall hereafter inhabit it. May none but honest and wise Men ever rule under this roof."

Thomas Jefferson

Banner commemorating Jefferson's election, 1800

Thomas Jefferson believed in a national government that had limited powers over the states and the people. Yet, as president, he made bold decisions for the country. In 1803, he purchased the vast territory of Louisiana from France for 15 million dollars. This doubled the size of the country and made westward expansion possible. Jefferson kept the nation neutral during the Napoleonic Wars. After eight years as president, he stepped down.

Jefferson the patriot

A brilliant lawyer, Jefferson was elected to the Virginia House of Burgesses at age 25. At the start of the Revolutionary War, he served in the Continental Congress, which acted on behalf of the colonies. He was also elected governor of Virginia. In 1784, he went to Europe, joining John Adams and Benjamin Franklin, to negotiate treaties with European powers. Jefferson returned in 1789 to take up his role as secretary of state. In 1801, he became president.

Jefferson (right) writing the Declaration of Independence with John Adams (center) and Benjamin Franklin (left)

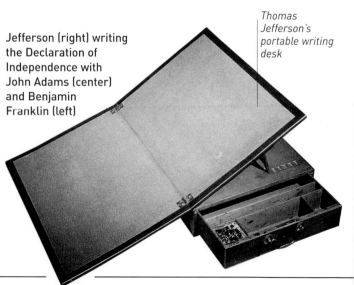

Thomas Jefferson's portable writing desk

The Declaration of Independence

At the Continental Congress in 1776, Thomas Jefferson was asked to write the Declaration of Independence. In this historic document, he stated the belief that all people had certain basic rights to life and liberty that no government could take away. The Declaration was addressed to the British king, George III, whom the Americans accused of stepping on their rights and freedoms. They argued that the American colonies should be "free and independent states."

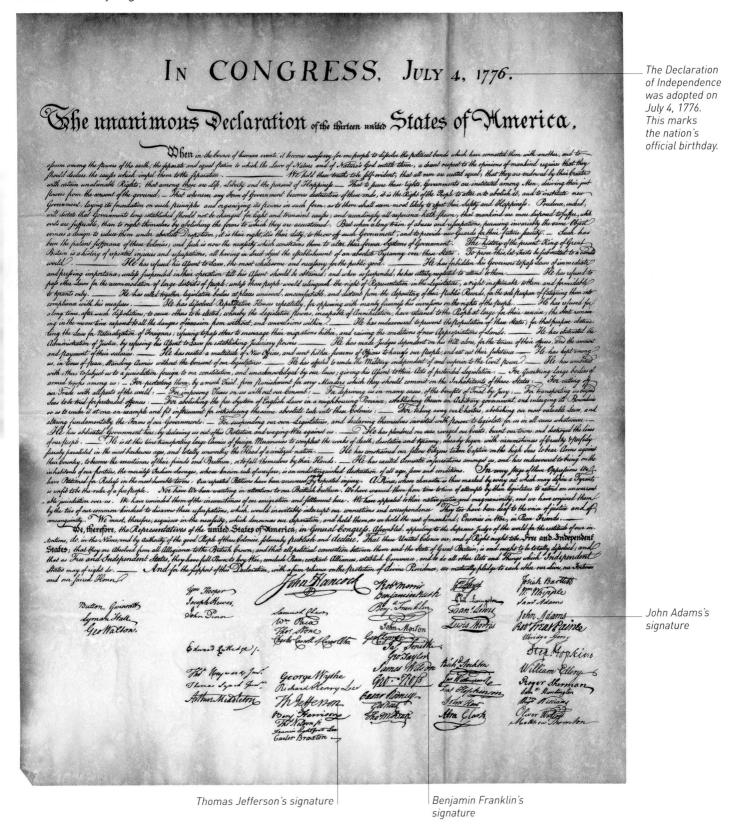

The Declaration of Independence was adopted on July 4, 1776. This marks the nation's official birthday.

John Adams's signature

Thomas Jefferson's signature

Benjamin Franklin's signature

Continued on next page

Great scholar

Thomas Jefferson was one of the most learned men in American history. He knew six languages, studied music, law, science, and philosophy, and was a self-taught architect. At age 33, he wrote the Declaration of Independence. He also championed religious freedom and public education, dispatched an expedition to discover the natural wonders of the continent, and pioneered neoclassical architecture in the United States.

Monticello

One of Jefferson's many interests was architecture. Inspired by 16th-century Italian architect Andrea Palladio, he designed his home on a hill above Charlottesville, Virginia. He named it Monticello, Italian for "little mountain." The 32-room house was the embodiment of Jefferson's classical tastes. He designed many features for Monticello, such as a dumbwaiter in which food could be raised from the cellar, swivel chairs, and alcove beds.

The University of Virginia

Jefferson believed strongly in education, in part so that citizens could make informed decisions about public affairs. One of his proudest achievements was founding the University of Virginia. He planned the curriculum and even designed the buildings.

Colonnaded buildings designed by Jefferson

Sacagawea became a heroine in national folklore.

Jefferson and religion

Jefferson wrote his own interpretation of the New Testament to better understand what he thought were the true teachings of Jesus. He is remembered for his ardent support of religious freedom. As a member of the Virginia legislature in the 1770s, he fought for a statute of religious freedom, which was accepted in 1786.

The Jefferson Bible

Jefferson's gravestone

Final resting place

Thomas Jefferson died on July 4, 1826, a few hours before John Adams. He was laid to rest at Monticello. He left an epitaph for his gravestone: "Here was buried Thomas Jefferson, Author of the Declaration of Independence, of the Statute of Virginia for Religious Freedom, and the Father of the University of Virginia." He did not mention that he had been president.

The Lewis and Clark Expedition

Jefferson was an avid amateur naturalist, and he was eager to find out about the American interior. In 1804, he sent an expedition, led by Meriwether Lewis and William Clark, to explore the newly acquired Louisiana Territory. Lewis and Clark were aided by a Shoshone girl named Sacagawea, who helped them communicate with the different Native American peoples they met. Over two years, the expedition members traveled as far as the Pacific Ocean. They kept detailed accounts of the plants, animals, and birds they saw, and mapped the natural features of the continent.

This is the compass carried by the explorers on the Lewis and Clark Expedition.

Meriwether Lewis was appointed governor of the Louisiana Territory upon his return in 1806.

William Clark became superintendent of Indian affairs in the Louisiana Territory and, later, governor of the Missouri Territory.

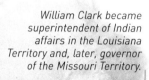

Thomas Jefferson

3RD PRESIDENT
1801–1809

BORN
April 13, 1743
Albemarle County, Virginia

INAUGURATED AS PRESIDENT
First term: March 4, 1801
Second term: March 4, 1805

AGE AT INAUGURATION
57

PARTY
Democratic-Republican

WIFE
Martha Wayles Skelton
(died 1782)

CHILDREN
Martha
Mary
Lucy Elizabeth

DIED
July 4, 1826
Charlottesville, Virginia

KEY EVENTS OF PRESIDENCY

1801 Jefferson sends the Navy to quell the Barbary pirates in the Mediterranean.

1803 In the Marbury v. Madison case, the Supreme Court declares an act of Congress to be unconstitutional for the first time; Jefferson makes the Louisiana Purchase.

1804 Jefferson is reelected as president; Jefferson's rival, Aaron Burr, kills Alexander Hamilton in a duel; the Lewis and Clark Expedition sets off.

1806 Aaron Burr tries to incite a rebellion in Louisiana.

1807 Burr is arrested and tried for treason, but is acquitted; the US frigate *Chesapeake* is fired upon and boarded by the British warship *Leopard*—Jefferson sticks to his policy of neutrality and avoids a declaration of war; Jefferson signs the Embargo Act banning the export of US goods to Europe in retaliation for the *Chesapeake* incident.

1808 Jefferson prohibits the import of slaves from Africa.

James Madison

James Madison was a great political thinker. In 1787, he was a leader in framing the Constitution and was nicknamed the "Father of the Constitution." After serving as Jefferson's secretary of state for eight years, Madison became president in 1809. During his administration, the United States became involved in the War of 1812 with Great Britain. The war went badly for the US and people referred to it bitterly as "Mr. Madison's War." Madison's reputation was rescued, in part, when US troops under General Andrew Jackson won a brilliant victory at the Battle of New Orleans in 1815.

The Bill of Rights

In the 1780s, Madison led the fight to have safeguards built into the Constitution. These took the form of the first 10 amendments, known as the Bill of Rights. Adopted in 1791, it guaranteed freedom of speech, religion, and assembly, and the right to trial by jury.

In stature, James Madison was the nation's smallest president. Barely 5 ft 6 in (1.6 m) tall, he weighed only about 100 lb (45.3 kg).

Mr. Madison's war

In June, 1812, a group of politicians known as the War Hawks persuaded the president to declare war on Great Britain. There were reasons for the war—British harassment of US ships and the kidnapping of American sailors—but Madison was reluctant. His country was ill-prepared to fight, and the war went badly for the US.

Washington in flames

1814 was a bleak year for President Madison. In August, British forces burned the capital, Washington, D.C. A peace treaty was signed later that year, but neither the US nor Great Britain could be said to have won the war.

The British Army lost three generals at the Battle of New Orleans in 1815.

A plucky first lady

Dolley Madison was a popular first lady who also knew how to keep her head in a crisis. When the British invaded Washington, D.C., Dolley was told to flee the White House. She packed up her husband's papers, the national seal, and a portrait of George Washington, and sent them on ahead before leaving. Shortly after, British troops set fire to the White House.

James Monroe

James Monroe was the last of the Revolutionary Patriots to become president. He helped negotiate the Louisiana Purchase and served as secretary of state and secretary of war under Madison. Monroe's presidency was known as the "Era of Good Feelings," because the nation was at peace. Yet not everything was ideal. There was a depression in 1819, and the Missouri Compromise of 1820 ignited debates about the extension of slavery in the new states and territories. Monroe is best remembered, though, for his foreign policy doctrine.

Monroe's own handwritten draft of the Monroe Doctrine

Serious by nature, Monroe proved to be a popular president.

The Monroe Doctrine

In 1823, President Monroe declared that the United States would not look kindly on European nations that interfered in North and South American affairs, or tried to establish colonies in the Americas. This was known as the Monroe Doctrine.

John Quincy Adams

John Quincy Adams was the son of former president John Adams. Like his father, John Quincy Adams had a sober personality. His good education and talent for learning languages contributed to his great success as a diplomat. Yet, as president, Adams was not as successful. He found that the people were not interested in his advanced ideas for spending their taxes on internal improvements—roads and canals—and scientific explorations. Adams was not reelected.

Portrait of John Quincy Adams painted in 1844

Death in the House

After losing reelection in 1828, John Quincy Adams embarked on a distinguished career in the House of Representatives, where he was a vigorous opponent of slavery. In 1848, at age 80, Adams suffered a stroke and died two days later. His last words were: "Thank the officers of the House. This is the last of earth. I am content."

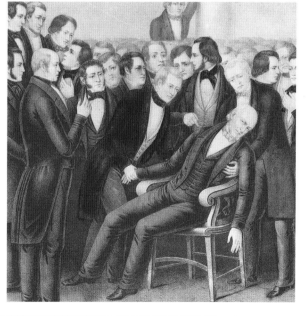

Microscope belonging to the scholarly John Quincy Adams

James Madison

4TH PRESIDENT
1809–1817
BORN
March 16, 1751, Port Conway, Virginia
DIED
June 28, 1836, Montpelier, Virginia

James Monroe

5TH PRESIDENT
1817–1825
BORN
April 28, 1758, Westmoreland County, Virginia
DIED
July 4, 1831, New York City, New York

John Quincy Adams

6TH PRESIDENT
1825–1829
BORN
July 11, 1767, Quincy, Massachusetts
DIED
February 23, 1848, Washington, D.C.

Andrew Jackson

Andrew Jackson was the first president born in a log cabin, and he brought a frontier spirit to the White House. He believed it was his job to represent ordinary citizens and vetoed legislation that favored the wealthy, a policy known as "Jacksonian democracy." A popular president, Jackson was easily reelected.

Pot metal statuette of General Jackson

Woman's decorative comb bearing Jackson's image

Snuff box shows Jackson as a war hero

Inauguration Day antics

Wealthy politicians in Congress thought Jackson's election would be the beginning of mob rule. Events on Inauguration Day seemed to confirm their fears. Rowdy supporters crowded into the White House to celebrate, and Jackson was forced to flee.

Andrew Jackson

7TH PRESIDENT
1829–1837

BORN
March 15, 1767
The Waxhaws, South Carolina

INAUGURATED AS PRESIDENT
First term: March 4, 1829
Second term: March 4, 1833

AGE AT INAUGURATION
61

PARTY
Democratic

WIFE
Rachel Donelson Robards
(died 1828)

ADOPTED
Andrew Jackson Jr.

DIED
June 8, 1845
Nashville, Tennessee

A battlefield hero as president

Andrew Jackson was born into poverty. His Irish father died before he was born and the young Jackson lost his mother when he was 15. Despite receiving little education, Jackson became a prosperous planter and judge in Tennessee. He also enjoyed a legendary military career, earning the nickname "Hero of New Orleans" for defeating the British Army in the War of 1812.

Jackson was a tall, commanding man and cut a dashing figure.

Jackson is dressed in the blue general's coat that he may have worn at the Battle of New Orleans.

All 183 of the Texas rebels were killed.

King Andrew

Many politicians thought Jackson abused his position of power in the name of the people. In their opinion, he too often vetoed legislation as he saw fit, rather than giving in to the will of Congress. His enemies named him "King Andrew," implying that he behaved more like a king than an elected president.

Cartoon portrays Jackson as a king with a scepter in one hand and a document declaring his power of veto in the other

The Alamo

When Jackson became president, Texas belonged to Mexico, although he was eager for it to join the Union. The president's wish was in part fulfilled in 1835 and 1836. When Mexico outlawed slavery in Texas, the white settlers were furious. A group of them captured San Antonio, but the Mexicans sent in the army. The siege of the Alamo began, and the rebels were killed. Six weeks later, the Texans defeated the Mexicans and won independence. The territory could now join the Union.

Dueling pistols c.1800

Daring duels

By nature, Andrew Jackson was temperamental and sensitive to insults. He once shot and killed a man in a duel over an unkind remark about his wife, Rachel.

Forcing the Indians west

Jackson had fought in the war with the Creek Indians. The Creeks called him "Sharp Knife," a name he lived up to. He signed the Indian Removal Act (1830). This allowed the government to remove Native Americans forcibly from their homelands to the frontier.

Gold epaulettes

Dance wand from the Cherokee, whose land in Georgia was confiscated by Jackson's government

This humorous 1834 biography of Jackson satirizes the president. It purports to be written by a Major Jack Downing, but was really the work of humorist Seba Smith of New England.

The Hermitage

A prosperous planter, Jackson lived in a mansion near Nashville called the Hermitage. Jackson and his wife, Rachel, are buried in the garden.

A photograph, or daguerrotype, of Van Buren in later years

Martin Van Buren

Martin Van Buren inspired many nicknames, most of which alluded to his political cunning. Called the "Little Magician," he was also compared to a fox. Van Buren had been Andrew Jackson's trusted vice president. Jackson chose him to be the next president, and the voters supported Jackson's choice. Unfortunately, an economic depression followed Van Buren to the White House. When he was unable to bring back prosperity, he was voted out of office.

Champagne-drinking president

President Van Buren had expensive tastes, for which he was sometimes criticized. During the election campaign of 1840 against William Henry Harrison, Van Buren was portrayed as an irresponsible dandy who dressed himself in finery while the country was in the midst of an economic depression.

Van Buren smiles when he sips champagne...

Campaign item from the 1840 election

... and frowns when he tastes common cider!

Trail of Tears

Van Buren continued Andrew Jackson's Indian removal policies. Between 1838 and 1839, 15,000 Cherokee were escorted by federal troops from their Georgia homeland to reservations in what is now Oklahoma. They were forced to march without rest, and many died along the way. Their journey became known as the Trail of Tears.

About 4,000 Cherokee died on the 116-day journey.

The Cherokee were forced to travel in the bitter cold of fall and winter with inadequate supplies of food.

William Henry Harrison

William Henry Harrison was born on a plantation in Virginia. His father had signed the Declaration of Independence and his grandson, Benjamin Harrison, would later become president. Harrison was a military hero. In 1811, he defeated Chief Tecumseh and his Shawnee warriors at the Battle of Tippecanoe in the Indiana Territory. Harrison is, however, remembered largely for serving the shortest term of any president.

Harrison was the first president to die in office.

Log cabin campaign
In the election of 1840, Harrison's supporters led people to believe their candidate had grown up poor in a log cabin, instead of in a mansion. This was the famous "log cabin and hard cider campaign."

President's deathbed
Sixty-eight-year-old Harrison developed pneumonia after delivering the longest inaugural address ever on a bitterly cold March day. Doctors fought to save the president, but he died on April 4, exactly one month to the day after his inauguration.

Martin Van Buren

8TH PRESIDENT
1837–1841

BORN
December 5, 1782, Kinderhook, New York

DIED
July 24, 1862, Kinderhook, New York

William Henry Harrison

9TH PRESIDENT
1841

BORN
February 9, 1773, Berkeley, Virginia

DIED
April 4, 1841, Washington, D.C.

John Tyler

10TH PRESIDENT
1841–1845

BORN
March 29, 1790, Charles City County, Virginia

DIED
January 18, 1862, Richmond, Virginia

John Tyler

Upon Harrison's death, John Tyler became the first vice president to become president. He belonged to the Whig Party, yet did not support many of the Whigs' policies, such as a national bank, federally funded roads and canals, and high tariffs to protect northern industries. Worse still, Tyler supported slavery, which many Whigs denounced. He became an outcast in his own party. Many of Tyler's critics challenged his right to call himself president because he had not been elected. His nickname was "His Accidency."

A true president
Tyler set a precedent for future vice presidents who became president, exercising all the powers and privileges of the office.

The new Mrs. Tyler
John Tyler was the first president to be married while in office. In 1844, he married the young and vivacious Julia Gardiner, who was 30 years his junior.

James K. Polk

Polk's eyeglasses

James K. Polk, a Democrat, was a former speaker of the House of Representatives and a governor of Tennessee. Polk believed that the United States should fulfill its "manifest destiny" of expanding to the Pacific Ocean. In 1846, a border dispute in Texas triggered a war with Mexico. At the Treaty of Guadalupe Hidalgo (1848), the victorious Americans acquired California and New Mexico. In the Pacific Northwest, Polk settled a long dispute with Great Britain over the Oregon Territory. When he left office, the country spanned two oceans.

James K. Polk

11TH PRESIDENT
1845–1849

BORN
November 2, 1795
Mecklenburg County,
North Carolina

INAUGURATED AS PRESIDENT
March 4, 1845

AGE AT INAUGURATION
49

PARTY
Democratic

FIRST LADY
Sarah Childress

CHILDREN
None

DIED
June 15, 1849
Nashville,
Tennessee

The Mexican War
President Polk tried to buy the southwestern territories from Mexico. When that failed, he instigated the Mexican War. The brilliant leadership of General Taylor and the US Army's superior weaponry led to Mexico's defeat in 1848.

1,000 Colt revolvers were issued to US soldiers in the Mexican War.

General Zachary Taylor's faithful horse, Whitey, was almost as famous as his owner during the Mexican War.

General Taylor

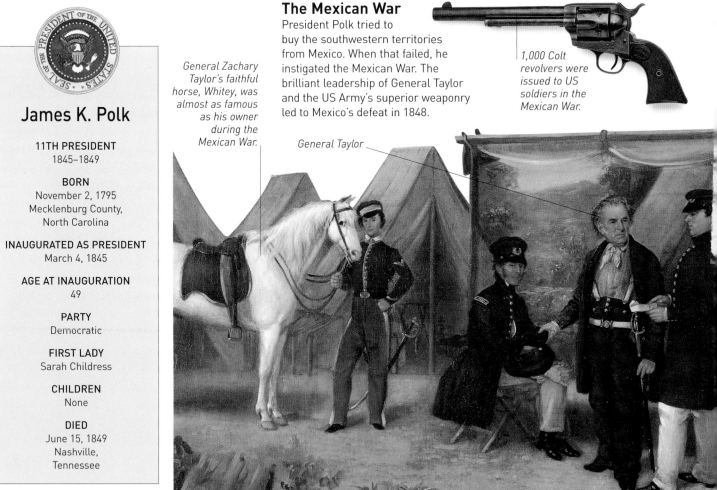

Zachary Taylor

Nicknamed "Old Rough and Ready," Zachary Taylor had no political experience. He won the election of 1848 mainly because of his popularity as a war hero. The extension of slavery in the new southwestern territories was the pressing issue of the day. Taylor did not want the new territories to become slave states. He threatened to veto the Compromise of 1850 because he thought that it favored the slave states. He died unexpectedly that year.

Although he looks sharp in this portrait, Taylor was often dressed in rumpled clothes and was said to look more like a farmer than a man destined for the White House.

California gold miners were called Forty-niners.

California Gold Rush

When gold was discovered in California in 1848 and 1849, thousands of prospectors poured into the territory hoping to make their fortunes. Taylor wanted California to enter the United States as a free (nonslave) state.

Buena Vista veteran

Zachary Taylor was a veteran of the War of 1812, the Black Hawk War in Illinois in 1832, and the Seminole War in Florida in 1836–37. He became a hero, though, for his victories in the Mexican War, most notably at the Battle of Buena Vista in 1847. There, he defeated the superior forces of General Santa Anna, losing only 700 men to the Mexicans' 1,500. Taylor's military successes earned him enormous acclaim. When he died in 1850, thousands of mourners lined the route of his funeral procession.

Taylor with members of his staff at his military encampment during the Mexican War

Zachary Taylor

12TH PRESIDENT
1849–1850

BORN
November 24, 1784
Montebello, Virginia

INAUGURATED AS PRESIDENT
March 5, 1849

AGE AT INAUGURATION
64

PARTY
Whig

FIRST LADY
Margaret Mackall Smith

CHILDREN
Ann Mackall
Sarah Knox
Octavia Pannill
Margaret Smith
Mary Elizabeth
Richard

DIED
July 9, 1850
Washington, D.C.

Millard Fillmore

Slave leg irons

Millard Fillmore grew up poor on a farm in New York state. He had little formal education, but was tutored by a young schoolteacher, Abigail Powers, whom he married. Zachary Taylor's vice president, he became president after Taylor's death. Fillmore favored the Compromise of 1850, which temporarily kept the Union together. By signing the Fugitive Slave Act, however, he lost the support of the northerners in his Whig party and was voted out of office in 1852.

Portrait of Fillmore, c. 1840

Perry's mission to Japan
In 1853, Fillmore sent Commodore Matthew Perry to open trade links with the Japanese, who refused to trade with other countries. Intimidated by US naval power, the emperor agreed to open Japan's ports.

The Fugitive Slave Act
The most controversial part of the Compromise of 1850 was the Fugitive Slave Act. It promised federal support for returning runaway slaves to their owners, allowing escaped slaves to be hunted down in the North. Abolitionists were outraged.

Uncle Tom's Cabin
Harriet Beecher Stowe was an abolitionist (someone who wanted to end slavery) from the North. She was horrified by the Fugitive Slave Act. In 1852, she published *Uncle Tom's Cabin*, a novel that showed the evils of slavery. Her book helped strengthen antislavery sentiments in the country.

Franklin Pierce

Just weeks before Franklin Pierce became president, his 11-year-old son, Benjamin, was killed in a train wreck. This sad event cast a shadow over his presidency. A New England lawyer, Pierce tried to keep peace between the North and the South, yet he made a fateful decision in supporting the Kansas-Nebraska Act (1854). This act left settlers to decide whether or not to allow slavery in their territories. It provoked fighting in what became known as "Bleeding Kansas." The country stepped closer to war.

Attack in the Senate
During the passage of the Kansas-Nebraska Act, southern representative Preston Brooks brutally attacked antislavery senator Charles Sumner.

Daguerrotype of Pierce, c. 1852; his nickname was "Handsome Frank."

Millard Fillmore

13TH PRESIDENT
1850–1853
BORN
January 7, 1800, Cayuga County, New York
DIED
March 8, 1874, Buffalo, New York

Franklin Pierce

14TH PRESIDENT
1853–1857
BORN
November 23, 1804, Hilsboro, New Hampshire
DIED
October 8, 1869, Concord, New Hampshire

James Buchanan

15TH PRESIDENT
1857–1861
BORN
April 23, 1791, Cove Gap, Pennsylvania
DIED
June 1, 1868, Lancaster, Pennsylvania

Bleeding Kansas
Abolitionists flooded into Kansas to vote in the Free-Soil (antislave) Party. But Kansas bordered Missouri, which was a slaveholding state. In 1855, thousands of Missourians crossed into Kansas to vote against the abolitionists. When a proslavery government was elected, a border war broke out.

"Border Ruffians" from Missouri

James Buchanan

The presidency of James Buchanan was doomed from the start. For 10 years, the slavery debate had troubled the occupants of the White House, and Buchanan was no exception. A lawyer, he argued that slavery was legal under the Constitution, and urged compromise. But the abolitionist movement was growing. Across the country, trust and reason were giving way to fear and anger. Buchanan became a spectator as events spun out of control. When he left office, war was inevitable.

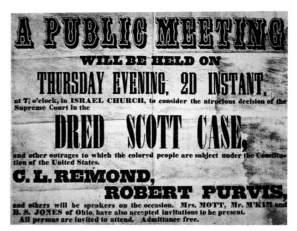

Buchanan, a courtly mannered bachelor, served in public life for 40 years.

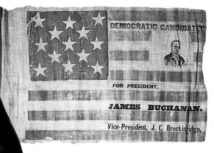

The Dred Scott decision
In 1857, the Supreme Court made a historic ruling in a case brought by a slave, Dred Scott. Scott sued for his freedom because he had lived in a free state and this made him free. The Court ruled that Scott was not a citizen and so could not file a lawsuit.

Campaign flag for Democratic candidate James Buchanan

John Brown's raid
John Brown was a radical abolitionist who, in 1859, attempted to start a slave rebellion. His aim was to capture the federal arsenal at Harper's Ferry, Virginia, and mount raids against slave owners. Brown was captured and hanged. Yet the legend of John Brown lived on.

Free-Soil activists in Kansas armed with a cannon

The Free-Soil cause
Buchanan urged Congress to accept Kansas as a slave state. In 1858, though, the proslavery constitution in Kansas was voted out. The Free-Soil Party joined the newly formed Republican Party, which promoted a strong antislavery platform in the 1860 election. That year, Republican candidate Abraham Lincoln was elected president. Kansas joined the Union as a free state in 1861.

Frederick Douglass
A former slave, Frederick Douglass was the foremost black abolitionist of his time. After John Brown's raid, President Buchanan sent agents to arrest Douglass. Douglass fled the country, but later returned.

Abraham Lincoln

Born in 1809, Abraham Lincoln grew up on the frontier, and later became a lawyer. He deplored slavery and spoke out against the evils of its expansion. In 1860, he was elected president. When the southern states left the Union, Lincoln faced a country on the brink of civil war. It became his mission to reunite the nation, an enormous task that no president, before or since, has faced.

Mary Todd Lincoln
Lincoln's wife Mary found her role as first lady difficult, and she was unpopular in Washington, D.C. Both the Civil War (she was a southerner) and the death of her son Willie in 1862 took a toll on her fragile mental health.

Lincoln's clothes often appeared ill-fitting, and his homely appearance sometimes provoked criticism.

OLD ABE,
ICH   MEIN.
PRINCE OF RAILS.

A wooden ax carried in campaign parades

Honest Abe
In the presidential campaign of 1860, Lincoln was presented as a good man who had worked his way to the top through honest labor. Lincoln was nicknamed the "Prince of Rails," in reference to an early job as a rail-splitter. Lincoln also worked as a ferryboat captain, a store clerk, a surveyor, and a postmaster before becoming a lawyer.

An unlikely leader
According to a close friend, Lincoln was driven by "a little engine that knew no rest." An ambitious young man, he was a self-trained lawyer and was later elected to the state legislature of Illinois. He was a member of Congress, and in 1860, became the Republican presidential candidate. Although he became one of the greatest presidents in American history, Lincoln did not cut a dashing figure. At 6 ft 4 in (1.9 m), he often appeared awkward, and spoke with a "frontier" accent.

Lincoln and slavery

The South relied on slave labor to produce the rice, cotton, and sugarcane on which its economy depended. Although Lincoln regarded slavery as unjust, he did not want to force the South to abolish it. But he did want to prevent new territories in the West from becoming slave states. Many southerners believed this signaled the end of slavery and their way of life.

Many slaves escaped to the free states in the North via the Underground Railroad, a system of safe houses operated by abolitionists.

A group of runaway slaves

Abraham Lincoln

16TH PRESIDENT
1861–1865

BORN
February 12, 1809
Hardin County, Kentucky

INAUGURATED AS PRESIDENT
First term: March 4, 1861
Second term: March 4, 1865

AGE AT INAUGURATION
52

PARTY
Republican

FIRST LADY
Mary Todd

CHILDREN
Robert Todd
Edward Baker
William Wallace
Thomas (Tad)

DIED
April 15, 1865
Washington, D.C.

KEY EVENTS OF PRESIDENCY

1861 Eleven southern states secede from the Union to create the Confederate States of America; Jefferson Davis is elected president of the Confederacy; Civil War erupts when Confederates fire on Fort Sumter; the Union Army is defeated at the first battle at Bull Run.

1862 The Confederates are stopped at Antietam; the Union Army is defeated at Fredericksburg.

1863 Lincoln issues his Emancipation Proclamation, freeing all slaves in areas of rebellion; the Confederates are defeated at Gettysburg; Ulysses S. Grant wins at Vicksburg.

1864 Grant is made commander of the Union forces; Lincoln is reelected unanimously; Union forces march through Georgia; the Confederates abandon Atlanta.

1865 The Union Army captures Richmond; General Lee surrenders at Appomattox; Lincoln is assassinated.

THE
UNION
IS
DISSOLVED!

Passed unanimously at 1.15 o'clock, P. M., December 20th, 1860.

AN ORDINANCE

To dissolve the Union between the State of South Carolina and other States united with her under the compact entitled "The Constitution of the United States of America."

CHARLESTON
MERCURY
EXTRA

The Union collapses

In 1867, rather than accept Lincoln as their president, most southern states chose to secede, or separate, from the Union. Lincoln did not believe the South had a constitutional right to secede. He had sworn to uphold the laws of the land and was determined to reunite the country, even if it meant war.

South Carolina was the first state to secede. This extra from the Charleston Mercury newspaper announces that decision.

Jefferson Davis

In February 1861, delegates from the Confederate states met in Montgomery, Alabama, to elect a president. They chose Jefferson Davis of Mississippi. Davis had entered Congress in 1845 and was a commander in the Mexican War. He served in the Senate and was secretary of war under President Pierce. Davis was a slave owner and supported the continuation of slavery.

A nation divided

In 1861, South Carolina, Georgia, Florida, Alabama, Mississippi, and Louisiana formed a new nation, the Confederate States of America. A week after Lincoln was inaugurated, the Confederate States adopted a constitution. Eleven states (purple) left the Union (green). Five border states (orange) remained, although some of their citizens backed the Confederacy.

The Civil War

On April 12, 1861, Confederates fired on Fort Sumter, a Union stronghold in Charleston, South Carolina. After 34 hours of bombardment, the soldiers of the Union garrison were forced to evacuate. The attack was a near-bloodless beginning to the bloodiest conflict in US history. The vicious fighting was to last four agonizing years. Lincoln was deeply pained by the bloodshed and could be seen pacing the streets of Washington, D.C., late at night. But he never lost faith, and under his leadership, the Union prevailed.

"Stars and Bars" Confederate flag

Accurate guns with rifled, or grooved, barrels were used in war for the first time, resulting in heavy casualties.

Confederate uniform cap, called a kepi

Abraham Lincoln and General George B. McClellan at the battlefield of Antietam, Maryland, October 3, 1862

This bullet-torn Confederate jacket was found on the battlefield of Seven Pines, Virginia.

On the battlefield

The Civil War was America's most bitter conflict. Soldiers on both sides fought fiercely. Because of new weapons, losses were heavy. At the Battle of Gettysburg, more than 50,000 men died. Some 600,000 soldiers—two percent of the population—died in the war.

Union uniform kepi

Engraving portraying Lincoln as the liberator of the slaves

Grant and his generals

It fell to Lincoln to raise an army and find generals to lead it. He appointed and dismissed several generals. Meanwhile, the Confederates, under Robert E. Lee, won key battles. Finally, Lincoln appointed Ulysses S. Grant, and the North began to win.

General Grant

Freeing the slaves

With the Emancipation Proclamation of 1863, Lincoln freed slaves in the South. Slaves were Confederate property, and as commander in chief of Union forces, Lincoln could order the seizure of enemy property. He had no authority, however, to free slaves outside of the Confederacy.

The Gettysburg Address

In November 1863, Lincoln came to Gettysburg, Pennsylvania, to dedicate a Union cemetery at the site of the deadliest battle of the war. He pledged "that these dead shall not have died in vain—that this nation, under God, shall have a new birth of freedom—and that government of the people, by the people, for the people, shall not perish from the earth."

Copy of Lincoln's own draft of the Gettysburg Address

Photograph of Lincoln taken in 1865

The legendary southern general Robert E. Lee

Victorious northern general Ulysses S. Grant

Lee and Grant shake hands.

Lee surrenders

On April 9, 1865, Confederate general Robert E. Lee surrendered to Union commander Ulysses S. Grant at Appomattox Court House, Virginia. Lincoln's greatest wish was to secure "a just and lasting peace," with "malice toward none, with charity for all."

Lincoln is assassinated

On April 14, 1865, Lincoln attended a performance of *Our American Cousin* at Ford's Theater. Confederate sympathizer John Wilkes Booth snuck into Lincoln's box and shot him. Lincoln was taken to a nearby boardinghouse, where he died the next day.

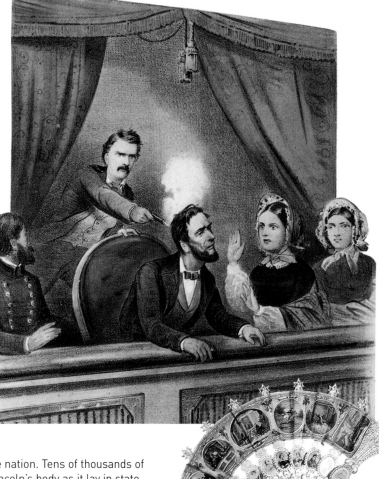

Sheet music for the funeral march

The nation mourns

The assassination stunned the nation. Tens of thousands of mourners viewed Abraham Lincoln's body as it lay in state. He was laid to rest on May 4, 1865, in Springfield, Illinois. The nation had lost a great leader at a time when he was still badly needed. Lincoln had not believed in punishing the South. With him gone, those bent on revenge gained influence.

Memorial fan of assassination

Andrew Johnson

Andrew Johnson was the only US senator from the South to remain loyal to the Union. For his steadfastness, he was nominated vice president in 1864. After Lincoln's assassination, Johnson became president. He tried to enact Lincoln's policy of leniency toward the South, but the "Radical Republicans" resisted. When Johnson refused to yield to their demands, he was impeached.

Vest made by Johnson

The Tennessee Tailor
Johnson was nicknamed the "Tennessee Tailor" because he began his working life as a tailor's apprentice. He received no formal schooling and his wife, Eliza, taught him how to read and write. By the age of 33, Johnson was elected to Congress.

Andrew Johnson

17TH PRESIDENT
1865–1869

BORN
December 29, 1808
Raleigh, North Carolina

INAUGURATED AS PRESIDENT
April 15, 1865

AGE AT INAUGURATION
56

PARTY
Democratic

FIRST LADY
Eliza McCardle

CHILDREN
Martha
Charles
Mary
Robert
Andrew

DIED
July 31, 1875
Carter County, Tennessee

Johnson in caricature
The Thirteenth Amendment freed the slaves, but African Americans were still denied the rights of citizenship. This cartoon depicts the president as Iago, from Shakespeare's *Othello*. He is giving false promises to Othello, who is shown as an African-American veteran. The satire is clear: Johnson is betraying black Americans.

Johnson portrayed as the traitor Iago

Political sketch shows former slaves being massacred

The president is impeached
In 1868, Andrew Johnson became the first president in history to be impeached, or put on trial, by the Senate. There were no constitutional grounds for prosecuting Johnson, just political disagreements over his postwar Reconstruction policies. Although he was spared removal from office by one vote, his presidency was all but over.

Members of the House of Representatives who prosecuted Johnson

Ticket for the impeachment trial of President Johnson

Ulysses S. Grant

18TH PRESIDENT
1869–1877

BORN
April 27, 1822
Point Pleasant, Ohio

INAUGURATED AS PRESIDENT
First term: March 4, 1869
Second term: March 4, 1873

AGE AT INAUGURATION
46

PARTY
Republican

FIRST LADY
Julia Boggs Dent

CHILDREN
Frederick Dent
Ulysses Simpson
Ellen Wrenshall
Jesse Root

DIED
July 23, 1885
Mount McGregor,
New York

Ulysses S. Grant

A war hero, Ulysses S. Grant became president in 1868, three years after the end of the Civil War. Unfortunately, he was ill-suited to the office. He unwittingly let dishonest people take advantage of him. After eight years, he was happy to leave the White House, saying he felt like a boy let out of school.

General Grant
The Civil War gave Grant the means to prove himself. He had been frustrated in several occupations—soldier, farmer, realtor—before becoming a Union general. On the battlefield, he was a dynamo.

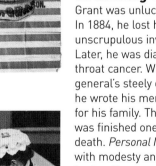

Paper lantern used in Grant's 1868 campaign

Campaign banner

Grant was 61 years old when this photograph was taken; he died two years later.

Grant's wife, Julia Boggs Dent

Grant surrounded by his family, 1883

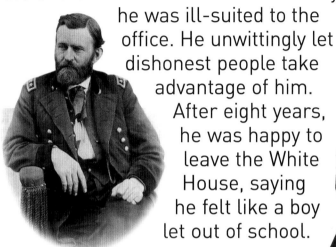

Soldiering on
Grant was unlucky in retirement. In 1884, he lost his savings to an unscrupulous investment broker. Later, he was diagnosed with throat cancer. With an old general's steely determination, he wrote his memoirs to provide for his family. The manuscript was finished one week before his death. *Personal Memoirs*, written with modesty and humor, was a best-seller.

General Grant with his horse during the Civil War; a shy man, Grant had always loved horses.

Rutherford B. Hayes

Like Ulysses S. Grant, Rutherford B. Hayes was a Union general in the Civil War. In 1877, he won a controversial election by one vote. Congress decided the contest, which left many of Hayes's opponents feeling cheated. They referred to Hayes as "His Fraudulency" and "Rutherfraud" Hayes. Hayes proved to be an even-handed, but unexceptional, president. He was lenient with the southern states and removed the last federal troops from their midst. By the end of his one term in office, Hayes had won over his critics.

Photograph of Lucy Hayes, 1878

This bust of Hayes, sculpted in 1876, was intended to convince voters that Hayes was a man of substance.

A political bargain

Hayes's opponent in 1876 was Samuel J. Tilden. When Tilden lost, southern Democrats threatened to secede. They declared that they would only accept Hayes as president if he agreed to remove federal troops from the South. He did.

Little Big Horn

In 1868, Congress deemed the Black Hills of South Dakota sacred to the Indians. But when gold was discovered there, it tried to remove the Indians. On June 25, 1876, a cavalry, led by George A. Custer, attacked the camp of Chief Sitting Bull on the Little Big Horn River. Custer's forces were routed, but the Indian victory was short-lived.

Lemonade Lucy

Lucy Hayes was the first college-educated first lady. She also backed the temperance movement. The White House banned alcohol, and Lucy was known as "Lemonade Lucy." She hosted the first Easter egg roll at the White House.

Edison telephone, 1879

First phone

Hayes was the first president to use a telephone in the White House.

Ceremonial eagle-feather headdress

Chief Sitting Bull led the Sioux, Cheyenne, and Arapaho warriors against Custer.

Little Big Horn River

Former Civil War officer, George A. Custer

James A. Garfield

Garfield was the third Civil War general to become president. The battlefield proved safer than the White House. Four months into his term, Garfield was shot by an assassin. He had wanted to reform the civil service system and the post office. He was the second president to be assassinated.

Memorial ribbon bearing Garfield's portrait

The assassin, Charles Guiteau

President Garfield

An assassin strikes

President Garfield was shot by Charles Guiteau, who was disgruntled because he could not obtain a federal job. Garfield survived for two months after the shooting. He died on September 19, 1881.

Rutherford B. Hayes

19TH PRESIDENT
1877–1881

BORN
October 4, 1822,
Delaware, Ohio

DIED
January 17, 1893,
Fremont, Ohio

James A. Garfield

20TH PRESIDENT
1881

BORN
November 19, 1831,
Orange Township, Ohio

DIED
September 19, 1881,
Elberon, New Jersey

Chester A. Arthur

21ST PRESIDENT
1881–1885

BORN
October 5, 1830,
North Fairfield, Vermont

DIED
November 18, 1886,
New York, New York

Chester A. Arthur

No one expected Chester A. Arthur to become president, but when Garfield was assassinated, Arthur took on the country's highest office. He continued to surprise his friends once he entered the White House. For years, he had been a "spoilsman," giving political jobs in return for his loyalty to the "Stalwarts" of the Republican Party. As president, he believed that politicians should earn federal jobs. In 1883, he signed the Pendleton Act, establishing the Civil Service Commission. Job seekers now had to pass exams. The Republican Party did not nominate him for a second term.

Chester A. Arthur was a fashionable dresser and was the first president to hire a valet.

Of the 200 US soldiers who followed Custer into battle, not one survived.

A Chinese worker flees from a gang of Irishmen.

Curb on immigration begins

During Arthur's term of office, racial tension in California between the Chinese and Irish was a problem. In a time of economic hardship, both groups were competing for the lowest-paid jobs, leading to street fights in San Francisco. In 1882, Congress passed the Chinese Exclusion Act, stopping Chinese immigration for 10 years.

Grover Cleveland

Grover Cleveland was the only president to serve nonconsecutive terms. He was ousted from office in 1889 by Benjamin Harrison, but returned four years later. President Cleveland was honest and hardworking. He believed in "hands-off" government and refused to favor individual groups. For instance, he vetoed what he thought were unnecessary pension bills for Civil War veterans. Cleveland vetoed more legislation than any president before him, earning the nickname "Old Veto." The Panic of 1893 plagued his second term. Although distressed by the plight of the unemployed, he did not believe in government intervention. He could not restore the economy and had to use federal troops to suppress labor unrest. He failed to win a third nomination.

Sheet music of Cleveland's wedding march

White House wedding

A highlight of Cleveland's first term was his marriage to Frances Folsom, the daughter of his former law partner. At 21, Frances became the youngest first lady. She was 28 years younger than Cleveland, and their marriage caused a stir. The charming, beautiful first lady became hugely popular, and her image was used in advertising campaigns.

Grover Cleveland

22ND PRESIDENT
1885–1889

24TH PRESIDENT
1893–1897

BORN
March 18, 1837,
Caldwell, New Jersey

DIED
June 24, 1908,
Princeton, New Jersey

Benjamin Harrison

23RD PRESIDENT
1889–1893

BORN
August 20, 1833,
North Bend, Ohio

DIED
March 13, 1901,
Indianapolis, Indiana

William McKinley

25TH PRESIDENT
1897–1901

BORN
January 29, 1843, Niles, Ohio

DIED
September 14, 1901,
Buffalo, New York

Man of destiny

The son of a poor Presbyterian minister, Cleveland received little formal education, but became a successful lawyer. In 1881, he became mayor of Buffalo, New York, where he made his name as a reformer. A year later, he was elected governor of New York. In 1884, he ran for president.

Federal troops battle with railroad workers.

Pullman rail strike

In 1894, a strike at the Pullman Car Company was interrupting mail service. Cleveland sent federal troops to break up the strike, and workers were forced to accept lower wages.

Cleveland campaign banner

Benjamin Harrison

Benjamin Harrison had deep roots in American history. His grandfather, William Henry Harrison, was the ninth president and his great-grandfather signed the Declaration of Independence. Harrison was a gifted public speaker, but those who met him often found him aloof. He supported the Sherman Antitrust Act of 1890—designed to regulate business and eliminate unfair practices, such as monopolies. However, he also signed the McKinley Tariff Act, protecting businesses from foreign competition by placing tariffs on imports. The result was a rise in prices that was unpopular. Harrison strengthened the Navy with a view to expanding US influence in Central America and the Pacific.

Immigration

In 1892, the government opened Ellis Island in New York to process the millions of immigrants arriving to the US from Europe. Most immigrants worked in the lowest-paid jobs and suffered hardship. Many workers became hostile to Harrison and to what they saw as his protection of big business. He was voted out of office in 1892.

Harrison was nicknamed the "Human Iceberg."

William McKinley

In the Civil War, the young William McKinley served under Rutherford B. Hayes, who later became president. In 1896, McKinley was elected to America's highest office. He favored a "hands-off" approach to economic affairs, and big business went unchecked. Best remembered for his foreign-policy successes, in 1898, he helped Cuba win its independence from Spain. By the Treaty of Paris in 1898, the US acquired Guam, Puerto Rico, and the Philippine islands. That year, it annexed Hawaii. Under McKinley, the nation became a global power.

Pictures of McKinley looking dour give the wrong impression. He was a warm and friendly man who charmed those around him.

President McKinley's Republican running mate in the 1900 election campaign was the then governor of New York, Theodore Roosevelt.

Assassin shoots McKinley

On September 6, 1901, William McKinley was shot by an anarchist in Buffalo, New York. The president died from his gunshot wounds eight days later.

The assassin hid his revolver under a bandage on his hand.

Theodore Roosevelt

When McKinley died in 1901, Theodore Roosevelt became the youngest US president, at age 42. A former writer and cowboy, he had held important political posts and was full of energy and idealism. Roosevelt wanted all Americans to have a "square deal."

Inauguration Day

Roosevelt enjoyed being president during his first term and was eager to continue. He was aware, though, that he had not been elected chief executive. His popularity was confirmed in 1904 by a solid victory.

A Rough Rider

When the Spanish-American War began in 1898, Roosevelt was assistant secretary of the Navy. He resigned and arranged to go to Cuba, which was struggling for independence from Spain. He raised a volunteer cavalry regiment called the Rough Riders and, in July, led a charge up San Juan Hill. The Spanish soon surrendered, and Roosevelt became a hero.

The White House Gang

The colorful first family caused mayhem. The young sons were nicknamed the "White House Gang" by the press. They had a menagerie of pets and would slide down the central staircase on trays. Daughter Alice enjoyed scandalizing the public. Her father reportedly said: "I can be president ... or I can control Alice. I cannot possibly do both."

A born rebel, Alice Roosevelt kept a pet snake and liked to smoke in public.

Edith Roosevelt presided over her eccentric family with calm and patience.

President Theodore Roosevelt with his family, 1903

Theodore Roosevelt

26TH PRESIDENT
1901–1909

BORN
October 27, 1858
New York, New York

INAUGURATED AS PRESIDENT
First term: September 14, 1901
Second term: March 4, 1905

AGE AT INAUGURATION
42

PARTY
Republican

FIRST LADY
Edith Kermit Carow

CHILDREN
Alice Lee
Theodore
Kermit
Ethel Carow
Archibald Bulloch
Quentin

DIED
January 6, 1919
Oyster Bay, New York

Protection for workers

Roosevelt believed that ordinary Americans should be protected against the might of industrialists. When coal miners in Pennsylvania went on strike for higher wages in 1902, he threatened to seize the mines unless the owners agreed to arbitration. He invited both sides to Washington, D.C. for discussions. The miners won many of their demands.

Teddy the crusader
Roosevelt was called the "Trust Buster" for his crusade against the unfair practices of big business. The tobacco, oil, steel, and railroad industries had formed trusts to keep prices high and wages low. He used legislation to curb their powers.

Cartoon shows John D. Rockefeller, head of the powerful Standard Oil Trust, about to swallow up Earth

Banner portrays Roosevelt as the protector of labor

A dinner invitation
Theodore Roosevelt believed in racial equality and was the first president to invite an African American to dinner at the White House. This 1901 lithograph celebrates his meeting with Booker T. Washington, principal of the Tuskegee Institute in Alabama and a renowned African-American educator.

Great outdoorsman

Roosevelt had a passion for the outdoors. He loved to go on hunting trips and safaris. At the time, hunting wild animals was accepted. As president, he created the first federal game reserves.

Once a cowboy
Roosevelt was a sickly boy. Yet he became a believer in strenuous exercise. After the death in 1884 of his first wife, Alice Lee, he became a cowboy in the Dakota Badlands. After two years, he returned to New York a tougher man.

Roosevelt's leather cowboy chaps

Cuddly brown "Teddy's bears" like this one soon became known as teddy bears, and have been beloved by children ever since.

Teddy's bear
On a hunting trip in 1902, Roosevelt refused to shoot a captured black bear. Cartoonist Clifford Berryman made this sketch for the *Washington Post*. "Teddy's bears" were soon being sold as toys.

Environmentalism
A farsighted environmentalist, Roosevelt believed that land, trees, and wildlife were resources not to be squandered. He established the first federal wildlife refuge in 1903. By executive order, he preserved millions of acres of forest and established the first five national parks.

Roosevelt stands with conservationists in front of the "Grizzly Giant" redwood in California.

William H. Taft

Taft was a good-natured man and did not mind being teased about his size; he even made jokes about it himself.

Weighing more than 300 lb (136 kg), Wlliam H. Taft was the largest president. His administration followed a progressive agenda, setting up the federal postal-savings system and passing the Sixteenth Amendment, which allowed for the collection of personal income tax.

Taft on a diplomatic mission to Japan as Roosevelt's secretary of war, 1905

First ball of the season

As a boy, Taft loved baseball. As president, he decided to throw the first ball on opening day of baseball season, creating a presidential tradition.

Baseball bat

Catcher's mitt and ball

An easygoing manner

Taft poses on a visit to Japan. Easygoing and gregarious, he was never pompous. After the dynamic Roosevelt, he failed to impress the public. When the two fell out in 1910, much of the press supported Roosevelt. On leaving the White House in 1913, Taft declared it "the lonesomest place in the world."

Campaign banner emphasizes the jowly, but friendly, face of "Big Bill"

"BILL"

Early Model T Ford

A new age arrives

Times were changing fast. Although Taft kept cows on the White House lawn, he also became the first president to buy an automobile for the White House.

Woodrow Wilson

Woodrow Wilson was awarded the Nobel Peace Prize.

Woodrow Wilson was a dynamic reformer, signing legislation to lower tariffs and regulate businesses and banks. He tried hard to keep the US out of World War I, but involvement was inevitable. When the war ended, Wilson helped to negotiate the Treaty of Versailles, but the Senate rejected it.

The second first lady

Wilson's first wife, Ellen, died during his first term in office. A year later, he was engaged to Edith, amid whispered criticism about the speed of his remarriage. After his stroke in 1919, Edith ran the White House. Many senators were dismayed by this "petticoat government," but the Wilsons continued in this way until the 1920 campaign.

A man of principles

A former professor and president of Princeton University, Wilson found it hard to compromise his moral principles, admitting, "I feel sorry for those who disagree with me." When the Senate rejected the Treaty of Versailles in 1919, he set off on a national tour to convince the people that his ideas were right. Exhausted from the Paris peace talks, he suffered a stroke three weeks into the tour.

President Wilson signing the Treaty of Versailles, June 28, 1919

World War I

Wilson struggled to keep the United States out of World War I. When Germany declared that US ships entering the waters around Great Britain would be attacked, he negotiated US neutrality. But, in 1917, Germany began forming an anti-American alliance. On April 2, Wilson asked Congress for a declaration of war. The US sent more than a million troops to Europe. They were a decisive factor in the collapse of Germany in October 1918.

Famous World War I army recruitment poster of Uncle Sam

The Treaty of Versailles

Wilson's Fourteen Points peace plan proposed "peace without victory." He wanted to create a League of Nations to help maintain peace. His European allies did not always agree with his lenient views toward Germany, and he had to make compromises. Still, the Senate rejected the treaty.

Prohibition arrives

In 1919, the United States went dry. Alcohol was seen as evil by religious groups and as the cause of poverty and crime by progressives. The Volstead Act and the Eighteenth Amendment made alcohol consumption illegal. It was the start of Prohibition, a time when illegal "speakeasy" bars and gangsters flourished.

A federal agent nails a "Closed" sign to a saloon door.

Suffragette button

Wilson votes for women

Women had campaigned for the right to vote since the mid-19th century. Wilson's support of the movement, along with women's involvement in the war effort, turned public opinion in their favor. In August 1920, the Nineteenth Amendment became law, granting women the vote.

Warren G. Harding

Warren G. Harding's campaign theme—"Back to Normalcy"—was a call for America to return to a simpler way of life after World War I. Voters liked it and elected Harding by a wide margin. In keeping with his unassuming nature, he yielded much of his executive power to Congress, which reduced taxes, raised tariffs, and put quotas on immigration. Unfortunately, Harding delegated authority to dishonest advisers, and scandals sullied his administration. In 1923, before he could be impeached for the wrongdoings of his advisers, he died suddenly, sparking rumors that he had been murdered.

A Harding campaign ribbon

Poker pals
Harding's trust in his advisers was evidenced by his habit of playing poker and drinking (which was illegal) with cabinet members, some of whom were later implicated in scandals.

Calvin Coolidge

Calvin Coolidge became president upon the death of Harding. Nicknamed "Silent Cal," Coolidge talked little and smiled less. Once, a society lady bet she could make him say more than three words at dinner. Coolidge replied, "You lose." Honest and restrained, Coolidge brought back a sense of trust to the presidency after the murky dealings of Harding's administration. The economy was in a period of great prosperity, and he saw no reason to interfere, believing that less government was best. Coolidge enjoyed afternoon naps and allegedly slept more hours than any other president.

Straight-laced Cal
Calvin Coolidge (center, with his cabinet, in 1924) was the son of a Vermont shopkeeper. A lawyer, he held several political posts before becoming governor of Massachusetts. Coolidge was a reserved man, but his upright values served him well in office.

Roaring Twenties
Coolidge's "hands-off" approach to the economy encouraged speculation in the stock market and led to an economic boom. A "live now, pay later" society emerged. Women found new freedoms: they cut their hair, wore shorter skirts, and danced the Charleston.

Amazing Grace
Grace Coolidge is pictured here with her tame raccoon, named Rebecca. The first lady was vivacious and enjoyed social gatherings. She was the perfect match for her dour husband. Their happiness was marred, though, when their youngest son died of blood poisoning in 1924.

Rebecca, the first lady's pet raccoon

The story of Lindbergh's Atlantic crossing was celebrated in numerous magazines and books.

The new aviators
On May 21, 1927, Charles Lindbergh made the first nonstop solo flight across the Atlantic. A thrilled Coolidge greeted him. The year before, Coolidge had signed the Air Commerce Act to regulate the aviation industry.

Herbert Hoover

A self-made millionaire, Herbert Hoover seemed to be a perfect choice for president. Unfortunately, only months after he took office, the stock market crashed, triggering the Great Depression. Banks ran out of money, businesses went bust, and people lost their jobs. Many blamed Hoover for the disaster. He tried to rally the nation, but he did not feel it was the government's job to provide welfare relief. He eventually gave banks and businesses federal loans, but did not help the destitute.

1928 Hoover button

The stock market crash

Fueled by overspeculation, the stock market crash of October 29, 1929, caused a downward spiral in the economy. Stock prices plummeted and businesses were ruined. The day became known as "Black Tuesday."

Ticker tape

News of the market collapse came by ticker-tape machine.

Success story

Despite being orphaned as a child, Hoover became a wealthy mining engineer. Voters of 1928 saw him as an American success story. Four years later, in the midst of the Depression, they had lost faith in him and he was not reelected.

Button urges voters to reelect Hoover

Warren G. Harding

29TH PRESIDENT
1921–1923

BORN
November 2, 1865,
Bloomington Grove, Ohio

DIED
August 2, 1923,
San Francisco, California

Calvin Coolidge

30TH PRESIDENT
1923–1929

BORN
July 4, 1872,
Plymouth Notch, Vermont

DIED
January 5, 1933, Northampton,
Massachusetts

Herbert Hoover

31ST PRESIDENT
1929–1933

BORN
August 10, 1874,
West Branch, Iowa

DIED
October 20, 1964,
New York, New York

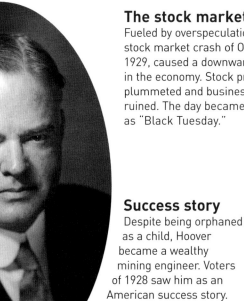

A shantytown of makeshift homes; such settlements became known as Hoovervilles.

SPEED UP RECOVERY
RE-ELECT
HOOVER
KEEP HIM ON THE JOB

Franklin D. Roosevelt

As president during the Great Depression, Roosevelt implemented revolutionary aid programs for banks, businesses, farmers, workers, and the unemployed. He empathized with the disadvantaged. Struck by polio in middle age, he could not walk unaided.

Eleanor Roosevelt
Eleanor married Franklin in 1905. As first lady, she drew her husband's attention to the needs of the poor. Her works of goodwill were an inspiration to Americans everywhere.

Like thousands of others, this destitute farm laborer set off on the road with his family looking for work.

The poor and hungry
Scenes such as this one became commonplace as the Depression deepened. The situation was made worse by a severe drought in the Great Plains. Millions suddenly had no work or money. Roosevelt pledged his help.

Pillow cover with anti-Prohibition message

21st Amendment
In 1933, Prohibition ended. The law had led to illicit bootlegging, smuggling, and the rise of gangsters.

A New Deal for all

Roosevelt called his program of aid and reform the New Deal. One of his goals was to put people back to work. He wanted to help what he called the forgotten man—the ordinary worker who was unemployed and hungry. He established federal programs for work projects and financial aid—solutions Hoover had refused to consider.

Sheet music for the rousing New Deal March

First friend

Roosevelt's black Scottie dog, Fala, accompanied the president everywhere and soon became a national celebrity.

Roosevelt talks to the nation

After the 1933 banking collapse, the president said: "The only thing we have to fear is fear itself," and temporarily closed the banks. In his first radio "fireside chat," he urged people to put their cash back into the banks. They did.

Reassuring radio broadcasts became an important aspect of Roosevelt's appeal.

In the 1930s, radio was the fastest way of communicating important news to the nation.

Continued on next page 41

Dr. Win-the-War

In 1940, Roosevelt won a third term. No president before had been in office longer than eight years. Roosevelt's leadership was still needed to pull America out of the Depression. But, on the heels of one crisis came another—World War II. Ironically, the war effort put an end to the country's economic woes. The US entered the war in December 1941, after Japan attacked the US naval base at Pearl Harbor. Over the next four years, Roosevelt set up programs for training the millions of people needed for the armed forces. With the Allied leaders Winston Churchill of Great Britain and Joseph Stalin of the Soviet Union, he planned strategies that would lead to the defeat of Germany, Italy, and Japan. In 1944, he won reelection so that he could see the war through to its end. But the war had taken a toll on his health. He died in April 1945, a month before Germany surrendered.

A new persona
With the start of hostilities, Roosevelt took on a new public persona. He declared that "Dr. New Deal" had to become "Dr. Win-the-War."

Pearl Harbor
On December 7, 1941, Japanese bombers carried out a surprise attack on US bases at Pearl Habor, Hawaii. More than 2,300 servicemen were killed, 1,300 wounded, and 1,000 unacccounted for. The attack destroyed 18 US ships and more than 200 aircraft. The president brought the US into World War II.

USS Shaw explodes as it is hit by a Japanese bomb in Pearl Harbor.

Albert Einstein became a US citizen and professor at Princeton University in 1940.

The Manhattan Project
In 1939, Roosevelt received word from the German scientist Albert Einstein that Germany might be developing an atomic bomb. After Pearl Harbor, he set up a research project and allocated it $2 billion. Work on the "Manhattan Project" took place at Columbia University in Manhattan. On July 16, 1945, the US detonated the world's first atomic bomb in the New Mexico desert.

This statue at Arlington National Cemetery is based on the 1945 photo by Joe Rosenthal. It shows the bravery and sacrifice of US Marines in World War II.

The home front

Once America had entered the war, millions were needed to serve in the armed forces. At home, this left many jobs unfilled. The government launched campaigns urging Americans to work for the war effort. Roosevelt put his energy into getting factories to retool for war production.

This poster contains the words of one of Roosevelt's morale-boosting speeches.

WE ARE NOW IN THIS WAR
We are all in it all the way

Every single man, woman and child is a partner in the most tremendous undertaking of our American history. We must share together the bad news and the good news, the defeats and the victories—the changing fortunes of war.

(President Roosevelt, Address to the Nation, December 9, 1941)

DEFEND AMERICAN FREEDOM
ITS EVERYBODY'S JOB

The Stars and Stripes was raised by Marines over the Pacific island of Iwo Jima after one of the last great battles of the war.

The image of Uncle Sam was used to encourage new recruits into the war industry.

The Big Three at Tehran, Iran, in November 1943

Joseph Stalin

Franklin D. Roosevelt

Winston Churchill

The Big Three

In November 1943, Roosevelt met with Churchill and Stalin. The "Big Three" discussed plans for a joint invasion of German-occupied France. Stalin wanted this to happen soon to take pressure off the Russian front, but the D-Day invasion did not take place until June 6, 1944. Headed by General Dwight Eisenhower, it led to the liberation of France and German defeat.

Many believed Roosevelt should not run for a fourth term. This campaign item stresses that he should continue.

THE DIFFERENCE between the **DEMOCRATS** AND **REPUBLICANS** IS **12 YEARS OF EXPERIENCE**

Victory in the Pacific

Iwo Jima was the scene of one of the Pacific war's hardest-fought battles, in February 1945. Almost 7,000 US soldiers were lost in the four-day struggle. Japan finally surrendered to the US on August 14, 1945.

Harry S. Truman

Harry S. Truman

33RD PRESIDENT
1945–1953

BORN
May 8, 1884
Lamar, Missouri

INAUGURATED AS PRESIDENT
First term: April 12, 1945
Second term: January 20, 1949

AGE AT INAUGURATION
60

PARTY
Democratic

FIRST LADY
Elizabeth (Bess) Virginia
Wallace

CHILDREN
Margaret

DIED
December 26, 1972
Kansas City, Missouri

Roosevelt's death in 1945 put Truman in the White House. The war in Europe was ending, but the Pacific war dragged on. The Japanese refused to surrender, and Truman did not want to risk more US lives. He ordered two atomic bombs to be dropped on Japan. Within days, the war was over. After the war, his "Fair Deal" bills proposed national medical insurance and a civil rights bill, but both were defeated in Congress.

The Trumans at home
Although he met his future wife at Sunday school at age six, Truman and "Bess" Wallace did not marry until 1919, when they were in their thirties. Here, Truman is seen in a cheery mood with his wife (left) and daughter, Margaret, (right) giving information for a census.

Man from Independence
Roosevelt was a hard act to follow. Truman, a plain-spoken former haberdasher from Independence, Missouri, sometimes appeared brash in comparison. One of his favorite sayings was: "If you can't stand the heat, get out of the kitchen." A sign on his desk read: "The Buck Stops Here." He shouldered the burden of office with determination.

President Truman   George C. Marshall

A mushroom-shaped cloud of smoke and dust rose five miles above Hiroshima.

Bomb

On August 6, 1945, the US bomber *Enola Gay* dropped an atomic bomb over Hiroshima, killing 100,000 people. Truman wrote, "We have discovered the most terrible bomb in the history of the world."

The Truman Doctrine

After World War II, Stalin established communist governments in Eastern Europe. In 1947, Truman announced his Truman Doctrine, which promised US support to countries fighting communists. That year, Secretary of State George Marshall proposed the Marshall Plan to help war-ravaged Europe. Stalin denounced the aid as a capitalist plot. The Cold War had begun.

Airlift

In April 1948, the USSR blockaded Berlin, Germany. The Soviets wanted to end the Allied presence in the city. Truman ordered supplies to be airlifted to Berlin. US and British supply planes enabled Berliners to survive until the blockade was lifted in May 1949.

1948 election campaign poster

★ BEAT HIGH PRICES ★

ELECT
HARRY S. TRUMAN
PRESIDENT
ALBEN W. BARKLEY
VICE-PRESIDENT

Against the odds, Truman was reelected in 1948, beating the favorite, Governor Thomas Dewey of New York.

Berlin children watch as an airplane brings in vital supplies.

US troops on the move in Korea

The Korean War

When communist North Korea tried to seize control of South Korea in 1950, fears of the spread of communism led Truman to send US troops into a country on the other side of the world. General Douglas MacArthur had orders to liberate South Korea. His invasion angered China, which sent vast numbers of troops. The war lasted until 1953.

Dwight D. Eisenhower

Eisenhower's eight years in the White House were years of peace and prosperity for most. He ended the Korean War in 1953 and tried to improve relations with the USSR by organizing cultural exchanges with Premier Nikita Khrushchev. These ended when a US spy plane was shot down in Soviet air space.

Likable Ike
"I Like Ike" was one of the most memorable campaign slogans of the 1950s. Eisenhower won a landslide victory in the 1952 election.

All-American first lady
Mamie was popular with voters. Her image as an all-American wife and mother was used to promote her husband as a family man.

"I Like Ike" buttons were worn everywhere—even by those who usually voted Democrat.

A 1956 campaign pail for Eisenhower and running mate Richard Nixon

These "Ike" golf tees from the 1956 Republican campaign promote the president through his favorite sport.

Dwight D. Eisenhower

34TH PRESIDENT
1953–1961

BORN
October 14, 1890
Denison, Texas

INAUGURATED AS PRESIDENT
First term: January 20, 1953
Second term: January 21, 1957

AGE AT INAUGURATION
62

PARTY
Republican

FIRST LADY
Marie (Mamie)
Geneva Doud

CHILDREN
Doud Dwight
John Sheldon

DIED
March 28, 1969
Washington, D.C.

Avid golfer
Eisenhower loved to play golf. He had a putting green and driving range built on the White House grounds, and was often seen there practicing his swing. Some senators thought he spent a little too much time trying to lower his handicap.

Eisenhower shakes hands with his five-year-old grandson David on a Georgia golf course.

The McCarthy hearings

In the 1950s, the US feared communist infiltration. Truman ordered an investigation of the government, which Eisenhower continued. Senator Joseph McCarthy of Wisconsin became notorious for conducting communist "witch hunts" in the State Department. His allegations ruined innocent people. Ultimately, he was ruined by his own slanders.

Senator McCarthy chuckles over an anti-McCarthyist advertisement in 1954.

Black students run the gauntlet of an angry mob as they try to enter school.

World War II general

Eisenhower was a good student at West Point, but not a great one. Few would have predicted his later success. In World War II, he led the European Theater of Operations. After invading North Africa and Italy, he was made Supreme Allied Commander in Europe and organized the D-Day landings. After the war, he became chief of staff, the army's highest office.

Eisenhower in his general's uniform

Little Rock

During Eisenhower's presidency civil rights became a pressing issue. After the Supreme Court ruled in 1954 that segregating black and white citizens was illegal, cities began desegregating their schools. In the South, there was strong resistance. In 1957, Governor Orval Faubus of Little Rock, Arkansas, called out the state's National Guard to prevent black students from enrolling in an all-white high school. Eisenhower sent federal troops to make sure the students were escorted safely to school.

Sputnik I

The Space Race

Americans were amazed when, on October 4, 1957, the Soviet Union launched the first satellite, *Sputnik I*, into space. Until then, American scientists had believed their space technology to be in advance of the Russians'. With Eisenhower's approval, Congress set up a new program to sponsor talented young scientists. The Space Race between the two nations had begun.

John F. Kennedy

Kennedy and his running mate, Lyndon B. Johnson, both supported the same civil rights goals.

At 43, John F. Kennedy was the youngest president ever elected. Kennedy brought youth and vitality to the White House. As part of his New Frontier program, he proposed civil rights legislation. He founded the Peace Corps, a way for young people to promote goodwill in developing countries. In 1961, he challenged the Soviet Union to put a man on the moon by the end of the decade. His term of office was tragically brief. In 1963, Kennedy was assassinated.

First lady of style

Jacqueline Bouvier married John Kennedy on September 12, 1953. They had three children: Caroline, John Fitzgerald Jr., and Patrick, who died in infancy. "Jackie" was attractive and charismatic. Her stylish wardrobe and elegant refurbishment of the White House brought glamour to the presidency.

Portrait of a president

Kennedy was born on May 29, 1917, into a large Irish-Catholic family. His father was millionaire tycoon Joseph P. Kennedy. After graduating from Harvard University in 1940, "Jack" joined the Navy. During World War II, he was decorated for heroism.

A new era

Kennedy was famous for his dynamic speeches. In his inaugural address, he said, "Ask not what your country can do for you— ask what you can do for your country."

Electioneering

Kennedy never lost an election. He enjoyed politicking, and, in 1960, ran for president with typical enthusiasm. Touting the slogan "Let's get this country moving again," he flew around the US in his own airplane, wooing voters with his charm.

President Kennedy greets supporters, 1962.

Fidel Castro of Cuba
Nikita Khrushchev

Cuban Missile Crisis

When Soviet nuclear missile sites were found in Cuba, Kennedy ordered a blockade of the island. For 13 days in October 1962, the US and USSR teetered on the brink of war. Soviet premier Nikita Khrushchev backed down. Ten months later, the US, UK, and USSR agreed to limit testing of nuclear weapons.

NONVIOLENCE...OUR MOST POTENT WEAPON

MARTIN LUTHER KING

Martin Luther King Jr.'s policy of nonviolence attracted huge numbers of supporters to his cause.

"I have a dream"

In August 1963, Martin Luther King Jr. delivered the now-famous speech to more than 200,000 marchers in Washington, D.C. He invoked the Declaration of Independence, saying: "I have a dream that one day this nation will rise up and live out the true meaning of its creed: 'We hold these truths to be self-evident, that all men are created equal.'" Kennedy's civil rights legislation was not passed until after his death.

Jackie Kennedy's quiet dignity at her husband's funeral moved the hearts of millions of television viewers.

President killed in Dallas, Texas

On November 22, 1963, Kennedy was riding through Dallas when an assassin opened fire. He was hit in the head and killed. Police arrested 24-year-old Lee Harvey Oswald, who was shot two days later by Jack Ruby while in police custody. The Warren Commission investigated Kennedy's death and concluded that Oswald acted alone.

America mourns

A grieving nation watched the televised state burial of John F. Kennedy at Arlington National Cemetery, Virginia, on November 25. Representatives of 93 nations came to pay their respects. Kennedy was president just 1,037 days.

This photograph of John F. Kennedy was taken moments before he was fatally shot.

John Connally, governor of Texas, was also wounded in the shooting.

Jackie Kennedy was not injured.

John F. Kennedy

35TH PRESIDENT
1961–1963

BORN
May 29, 1917
Brookline, Massachusetts

INAUGURATED AS PRESIDENT
January 20, 1961

AGE AT INAUGURATION
43

PARTY
Democratic

FIRST LADY
Jacqueline Lee Bouvier

CHILDREN
Caroline Bouvier
John Fitzgerald Jr.
Patrick Bouvier

DIED
November 22, 1963
Dallas, Texas

Lyndon B. Johnson

Lyndon B. Johnson became president after the tragic death of John F. Kennedy. A tall Texan, "LBJ" had grand designs for his country. He declared a "war on poverty" and tried to promote racial harmony, although race riots flared up, as did protests against the Vietnam War. A disheartened Johnson chose not to seek reelection.

Mrs. Johnson (left) and Jackie Kennedy (right) look on as Lyndon B. Johnson is sworn in as president within hours of JFK's death.

Johnson's dream

Johnson dreamed of a "Great Society," free of racial hatred and poverty. He was described by his opponents as ruthless and abrasive. Yet he was able to get his program of social legislation through Congress. The Civil Rights Act of 1964 banned racial segregation in public places and employment discrimination. The Voting Rights Act of 1965 outlawed the literacy requirement for voters. This rule had robbed many African Americans of their right to vote.

The LBJ family

It was a family tradition that all the Johnsons had the initials LBJ. Johnson called his dog Little Beagle Johnson. His children were Lynda Bird and Luci Baines, and the first lady was nicknamed Lady Bird. Her real name was Claudia Alta.

ALL AMERICANS MOVE FORWARD

"We have talked long enough in this country about equal rights. We have talked 100 years or more. It is time to write the next chapter, and write it in the books of law."

—President Johnson
November 27, 1963

Poster promoting Johnson's stand on civil rights

Sheet music for the Great Society March

Young antiwar protesters taunt the military police outside the Pentagon during a demonstration in October 1967.

The first US combat troops land at Da Nang, South Vietnam, March 11, 1965.

The Vietnam War

When Lyndon B. Johnson became president, about 16,000 American soldiers were in South Vietnam acting as military advisers to the government. They were trying to stop the communists in the North from taking over the entire country. The aggressive actions of the communists, however, soon led Johnson to order bombing raids. In 1965, he sent combat troops to protect American bases. Yet the conflict only escalated. By 1968, the United States had more than 500,000 troops in Vietnam. With American casualties mounting and no victory in sight, Johnson despaired of finding a quick and honorable end to the war.

Anti-Vietnam War poster of a battered Uncle Sam

Peace protests

"Make love, not war" became the rallying cry of America's youth. Antiwar protests gave rise to the Sixties' counterculture of hippies and "flower children." The Vietnam War cost Johnson dearly. Voted "Man of the Year" by *Time* magazine in 1964, by 1968, he was reviled.

In this 1967 cartoon, South Vietnamese leader Ky is sucking President Johnson's blood.

Richard M. Nixon

Few have known the highs and lows of politics like Richard M. Nixon. An able vice president to Eisenhower from 1953 to 1961, he lost a tight presidential race to Kennedy in 1960. Just as his political career seemed over, he was elected president in 1968. He had a flair for foreign diplomacy, witnessed the lunar landing, and brought an end to US involvement in Vietnam. Yet he is best known for the Watergate scandal. He is the only president to resign.

On his way up

After failing to win the presidency or the governorship of California, Nixon quit politics in 1962. He moved to New York to practice law. Before long, he was the Republican candidate in the 1968 election.

Nixon inaugural pennants

A match for Mao

Nixon sensed a rift between America's Cold War enemies China and the Soviet Union, so he opened negotiations with Chairman Mao. In 1971, Mao invited the US ping-pong team to China and Nixon went to Beijing for talks with Chinese premier Zhou Enlai. In 1972, he continued this policy of *détente*, or relaxation, by visiting Moscow. He announced plans for a US-Soviet program to limit nuclear arms.

Mao and Nixon hit a ping-pong ball, and opposing ideologies, in this cartoon.

Artist Norman Rockwell claimed Nixon was "the hardest man" he ever painted.

Early days

The son of a grocer, Nixon practiced law before joining the Navy in 1942. Elected to Congress in 1946, he was nicknamed "Tricky Dick" for his cunning in politics.

Buzz Aldrin photographed on the moon's surface by Neil Armstrong

"The Eagle has landed"

On July 20, 1969, the US put a man on the moon, fulfilling JFK's 1961 pledge. With the historic words, "One small step for man, one giant leap for mankind," US astronaut Neil Armstrong left the lunar module *Eagle* and stepped onto the moon's surface. President Nixon spoke with Armstrong and his fellow astronaut Edwin "Buzz" Aldrin during their moon walk. Millions worldwide watched the event on television.

Richard M. Nixon

37TH PRESIDENT
1969–1974

BORN
January 9, 1913
Yorba Linda, California

INAUGURATED AS PRESIDENT
First term: January 20, 1969
Second term: January 20, 1973

AGE AT INAUGURATION
56

PARTY
Republican

FIRST LADY
Thelma Catherine (Pat) Ryan

CHILDREN
Patricia
Julie

DIED
April 22, 1994
New York, New York

Nixon shakes hands with G.I.s of the First Infantry Division during his tour of Vietnam in July 1969.

"An American Tragedy"

IMPEACH NIXON !

Watergate

In June 1972, burglars were caught planting bugging devices in the Democratic Party headquarters at the Watergate complex in Washington, D.C. In the investigations that followed, Nixon denied involvement. However, witnesses testified that he had directed a cover-up of the Watergate affair and that he had taped all conversations held in the Oval Office. Nixon tried to avoid handing over the incriminating tapes, but, in July 1974, the tapes were heard. Articles of impeachment were immediately issued.

IMPEACH NIXON NOW 1974

Vietnam

To honor his campaign promise to end the Vietnam War, Nixon decided on a policy of "Vietnamization." This meant replacing US combat forces with South Vietnamese troops, while still providing air support and supplies. He stepped up bombings in North Vietnam and secretly started bombing enemy bases in neighboring Laos and Cambodia. The US signed a peace agreement with North Vietnam in January 1973. By March, all US combat troops had been withdrawn.

Nixon resigns

In a press conference in November 1973, Richard Nixon told the American people, "I am not a crook." Yet it soon became clear that Nixon had been involved in illegal activities. In August 1974, after a long, hard fight, Nixon was forced to resign or face impeachment proceedings. When he left the White House on August 9, Nixon forced a grin and gave his usual victory salute.

Nixon makes his televised resignation speech.

Gerald R. Ford

Gerald R. Ford's rise to the presidency was historic. Appointed vice president by Nixon after Spiro Agnew stepped down in 1973, Ford was sworn in as president in 1974 when Nixon resigned. He became the first president to hold office without having been elected. Ford announced: "Our long national nightmare is over." In a controversial gesture to heal the nation, he pardoned Nixon. He also gave amnesty to Vietnam deserters and draft-dodgers.

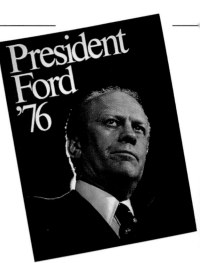

An eventful year
A highlight of Ford's two-and-a-half-year presidency was the 1976 Bicentennial celebration of the nation's founding. Later that year, Ford lost the presidential election to Jimmy Carter.

Football star
Ford went to the University of Michigan, where he enjoyed a dazzling football career. In 1941, he graduated in law from Yale University. Nicknamed "Mr. Nice Guy," Ford also had a reputation for being a patient thinker.

Gerald R. Ford

38TH PRESIDENT
1974–1977

BORN
July 14, 1913, Omaha, Nebraska

INAUGURATED AS PRESIDENT
August 9, 1974

AGE AT INAUGURATION
61

PARTY
Republican

FIRST LADY
Elizabeth Anne Bloomer

CHILDREN
Michael Gerald, John Gardner, Steven Meigs, Susan Elizabeth

DIED
December 26, 2006
Rancho Mirage, California

President Ford with his wife, Betty, and their family

A brave first lady
Betty Ford was a charismatic and outspoken first lady. She was a champion of women's rights and those of handicapped children. To help inform women about breast cancer, she publicized her own mastectomy. After her husband left office, Mrs. Ford bravely admitted to being an alcoholic and dependent on prescription drugs. With treatment, she recovered and went on to help found the Betty Ford Center in California.

Evacuation of Saigon
The peace treaty negotiated by President Nixon in Vietnam did not last long. In April 1975, communist forces captured the city of Saigon in South Vietnam. Prior to the invasion, hundreds of American citizens and Vietnamese refugees were airlifted to safety, bringing an end to US involvement in Vietnam.

Jimmy Carter

When Americans voted for Jimmy Carter, they were voting for change. People were tired of scandal-ridden politics and high inflation. But improving the economy proved harder than Carter had predicted. Nor could he ease the energy crisis. Americans soon regarded him as ineffective.

Carter bumper stickers

Peanut farmer
Carter grew up on a peanut farm near Plains, Georgia. After studying nuclear physics, he joined the Navy. When his father died, Carter returned to run the family business.

Jimmy Carter

39TH PRESIDENT
1977–1981

BORN
October 1, 1924
Plains, Georgia

INAUGURATED AS PRESIDENT
January 20, 1977

AGE AT INAUGURATION
53

PARTY
Democratic

FIRST LADY
Eleanor Rosalynn Smith

CHILDREN
John William
James Earl III
Jeffrey
Amy Lynn

Carter delivers Camp David Accord
In 1978, Carter played international peacemaker by hosting talks between President Sadat of Egypt and Prime Minister Begin of Israel. After nearly two weeks at Camp David, Maryland, both leaders signed the peace accords, ending the state of war between the two countries that had existed since 1948. Carter had achieved a stunning breakthrough.

Carter grapples with Iran
In November 1979, militant Iranians took the staff of the US embassy in Tehran hostage. They were angered by US support of the exiled shah of Iran. Carter's negotiations with Iran for the hostages' release failed. In April 1980, he approved a military rescue mission, but it also failed and eight servicemen died. The stalemate made him look ineffective in a crisis and shattered his reelection chances. The hostages were released in January 1981, on his last day in office.

1984 campaign belt buckle

Ronald Reagan

At 69, Ronald Reagan was the country's oldest president. A former actor, he was called the "Great Communicator" because of his ease on camera. His economic plan was to reduce taxes for the rich while cutting welfare programs. He believed that by supporting business, prosperity would filter down. He drastically increased defense spending and doubled the national debt. Still, he remained extremely popular.

Star quality
The son of a shoe salesman, Reagan started his career as a radio announcer. In 1937, he went to Hollywood, where he acted in more than 50 movies, including the 1951 *Bedtime for Bonzo*, above.

Assassination attempt
Shortly after he took office in 1981, President Reagan was shot. As doctors prepared to remove a bullet from his lung, the president joked, "I forgot to duck." Reagan made a remarkable recovery.

Reagan and Gorbachev pose for photographers in 1986

Cold War thaw
In 1985, Mikhail Gorbachev became leader of the Soviet Union and announced an era of *glasnost* (openness) and *perestroika* (restructuring). Reagan cautiously embarked on arms-control talks. In 1988, they both signed the Intermediate Range Nuclear Forces Treaty.

Painting of Reagan by Aaron Shikler that appeared on the cover of *Time* magazine in January 1981

Moments after this photograph was taken, the Challenger *space shuttle exploded, killing all seven astronauts*

Nancy Reagan launched a campaign to warn young people against the dangers of drug abuse

Shuttle disaster

The US space program experienced a huge setback when the *Challenger* space shuttle exploded shortly after liftoff on January 28, 1986. All seven members of the flight were killed, including teacher Christa McAuliffe, who had planned to broadcast classes from space. The "Star Wars" defense system also received bad publicity. It was meant to divert nuclear missiles away from the US using space-based lasers, but years of costly research produced little.

Lieutenant Colonel Oliver North arranged the money transfers to the contras. Here, he testifies before Congress.

Nancy Reagan

Born Anne Francis Robbins in New York City in 1923, Nancy Reagan was adopted as a child and took her stepfather's name, Davis. Using the stage name Nancy Davis, she became an actress. She became Ronald Reagan's second wife in 1952 and helped him in his political career. Although a popular first lady, she was criticized for her lavish tastes and for having too much influence on Reagan.

The Iran-Contra Affair

In November 1986, a scandal emerged that cast a shadow over Reagan's second term. A foreign press report revealed that the National Security Council had secretly, and illegally, sold weapons to Iran to try and secure the release of captive US citizens. The money from the arms deals was used to aid the anticommunist contras in Nicaragua—despite such aid being outlawed by Congress. In a television broadcast, Reagan declared that he knew nothing about these deals, but his credibility suffered.

Ronald Reagan

40TH PRESIDENT
1981–1989

BORN
February 6, 1911, Tampico, Illinois

INAUGURATED AS PRESIDENT
First term: January 20, 1981
Second term: January 20, 1985

AGE AT INAUGURATION
69

PARTY
Republican

FIRST LADY
Nancy Davis

CHILDREN
Maureen, Michael Edward, Patti Davis, Ronald Prescott

DIED
June 5, 2004
Los Angeles, California

George H. W. Bush

Foreign affairs dominated much of George H. W. Bush's presidency. In 1989, he ordered troops into Panama to oust corrupt dictator Manuel Noriega. A year later, he rallied a multinational coalition to force Iraq out of Kuwait. The collapse of the Soviet Union strengthened his image as the world's most powerful leader. Yet, as the country went into economic recession, Bush's popularity eroded.

Barbara Bush
Barbara Pierce married George H. W. Bush in 1945 and they had five children. Mrs. Bush used her role as first lady to become involved in charitable work. Her efforts made her very popular.

President Bush cheers on US troops during the Gulf War.

Win one, lose one
Bush was the first sitting vice president elected president since Martin Van Buren in 1836. But when he ran for reelection, he did not convince voters to stick with his conservative agenda.

Bush was Ronald Reagan's running mate in 1980 and 1984.

Saving the planet

Concerns about the environment and global warming were pressing issues in the 1980s. In his 1988 campaign, Bush promised to be the environmental president. In 1992, at the United Nations Earth Summit in Rio de Janeiro, Brazil, he signed the Earth Pledge, which required nations to limit the emission of greenhouse gases, monitor biodiversity, and work toward eco-friendly development. But he would not increase financial aid to developing nations to support their environmental goals.

Germans from East and West join hands along the Berlin Wall in front of the Brandenburg Gate.

East rejoins West at last

On November 9, 1989, East Germans began to tear down the Berlin Wall, which had stood for 28 years. This heralded the end of the Cold War. By 1990, Germany was reunified and communist governments in Eastern Europe began to collapse. There was now a "new world order."

The Gulf War

In August 1990, Iraq's leader, Saddam Hussein, ordered the invasion of oil-rich Kuwait. Bush coordinated a military coalition of US and allied forces against Hussein. In January 1991, the bombing campaign Operation Desert Storm was launched against Iraq. Six weeks later, the Iraqis were driven out of Kuwait by ground forces.

George H.W. Bush

41ST PRESIDENT
1989–1993

BORN
June 12, 1924
Milton, Massachusetts

**INAUGURATED
AS PRESIDENT**
January 20, 1989

AGE AT INAUGURATION
64

PARTY
Republican

FIRST LADY
Barbara Pierce

CHILDREN
George Walker, Robin,
John Ellis, Neil Mallon,
Marvin Pierce, Dorothy

Bill Clinton

The first US president born after World War II, Bill Clinton knew early on that he wanted to hold high office. At 32, he was elected governor of Arkansas—the youngest governor-elect. Fourteen years later, he entered the White House. As president, he enjoyed a time of peace and prosperity. In his first term, he negotiated the North American Free Trade Agreement and also secured peace in Haiti. Congress, however, refused to pass his health-care reforms. His second term was marred by scandal, but even this did not diminish his popularity.

The first family

Bill Clinton and Hillary Rodham first met at Yale University Law School. They married in 1975 and moved to Little Rock, Arkansas, in 1976, when Clinton was appointed state attorney general. They have one child, Chelsea, who was born in 1980.

A second term

Clinton and running mate Al Gore were reelected in 1996. Their victory was not a given, however, because the Republicans controlled both the House and the Senate.

A fateful encounter

In 1963, 16-year-old Bill visited the White House as part of a national conference of high school students. He shook hands with his hero, JFK. The encounter fueled his ambition to become president.

Foreign affairs

In July 1998, President Clinton committed US forces to a NATO operation to prevent ethnic cleansing in Kosovo (above). Part of the former Yugoslavia, Kosovo was inhabited mainly by ethnic Albanians. Thousands of Albanians were forced to flee as Serbian soldiers invaded. In 1999, Clinton agreed to support NATO air strikes against Serbia to halt the atrocities. The bombing forced the Serbs into submission. Kosovo declared independence in 2008.

Clinton gathers his thoughts before making a personal statement to the nation concerning his relationship with Monica Lewinsky.

Clinton confesses

In 1998, Clinton faced allegations about a relationship with a 21-year-old White House intern, Monica Lewinsky. He initially denied the allegations, but later admitted to a grand jury that he had had an "inappropriate relationship" with her. Impeachment proceedings on charges of perjury and obstruction of justice followed in January 1999. Clinton was acquitted.

Political family

No first lady has been as active in politics as Hillary Clinton. "If you elect Bill, you get me," she said in the 1992 campaign. In 2000, she became a US senator. She lost her bid for the presidency in 2008 and again in 2016.

Pin in the shape of Clinton's saxophone

Campaign button reads: "The cure for the blues"

Rhythm and Blues

A talented musician, Bill Clinton was offered music scholarships when he graduated high school. Instead, he chose to study politics at Georgetown University in Washington, D.C. As president, he, on occasion, played his sax for the public.

Clinton waits in the Map Room of the White House, August 17, 1998.

Bill Clinton

42ND PRESIDENT
1993–2001

BORN
August 19, 1946
Hope, Arkansas

INAUGURATED AS PRESIDENT
First term: January 20, 1993
Second term: January 20, 1997

AGE AT INAUGURATION
46

PARTY
Democratic

FIRST LADY
Hillary Rodham

CHILDREN
Chelsea

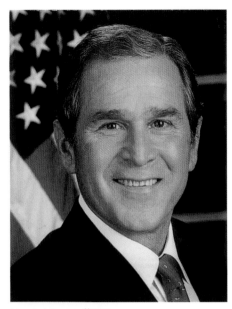

George W. Bush

Commemorative campaign toys

Like John Quincy Adams, George W. Bush was the son of a former president. Also like Adams, he was elected in a controversial election. Following the terrorist attacks of September 11, 2001, Bush launched a "war on terrorism." He sent troops to Afghanistan to hunt for Osama bin Laden and destroy al Qaeda. In 2003, he targeted the regime of dictator Saddam Hussein in Iraq. The unpopular war dominated his second term.

President "W"
To distinguish him from his father, the younger Bush was called "W." He liked to show his playful side—whether golfing with his father, jogging with his dogs, or hosting a kids' tee ball game at the White House.

2000 campaign button

A stylus is used to punch a hole for each vote.

Paper tabs, or "chads," sit along the center of the ballot.

Candidates' names are listed on both sides of the ballot.

The campaign trail
Bush was governor of Texas when he decided to run for president. He quickly gained financial and political support, but faced a tough race. He had to defeat the popular Senator John McCain for the Republican nomination, then battle Vice President Al Gore. Bush won a slim majority of the electoral vote, but not the popular vote. The fight over alleged miscounts in Florida went to the Supreme Court. He was declared the winner weeks after election day.

Chads

Voting machine
The 2000 election was hotly contested when ballots in Florida were miscounted by machines. Reviewers spent weeks recounting votes by hand to decide if each partial punch or "hanging chad" represented an intentional vote.

Impression from stylus

September 11

On September 11, 2001, Middle Eastern terrorists from the group al Qaeda hijacked airplanes to use as missiles. Two planes destroyed New York's World Trade Center, one damaged the Pentagon in Washington, D.C., and a fourth crashed in Pennsylvania. More than 3,000 Americans were killed. In response, Bush sent troops to Afghanistan to destroy al Qaeda and capture its leader, Osama bin Laden. National security became a priority, and prompted Bush to order the invasion of Iraq on March 20, 2003.

Bullhorn used to
address workers

Gas mask to protect
from smoke and ash

Suited up
On May 1, 2003, President Bush donned a flight suit and flew by Navy jet to the aircraft carrier USS *Abraham Lincoln*. There, he greeted 5,000 sailors, who had returned from a mission in Iraq.

Trade Center
New York saw the greatest destruction and loss of life from the 9/11 attacks with the fall of the World Trade Center's twin towers. Firefighters, police, and civilian volunteers worked around the clock to clear the site, which became a symbol of America's war against terrorism. Bush made several visits to the site to show support.

Rallying the troops
Bush visited military bases to rally soldiers leaving for Afghanistan and Iraq. His appearances served not only to encourage the troops, but also to seek approval from the American people and pressure Congress for more defense funds.

George W. Bush

43RD PRESIDENT
2001–2009

BORN
July 6, 1946
Midland, Texas

INAUGURATED AS PRESIDENT
First term: January 20, 2001
Second term: January 20, 2005

AGE AT INAUGURATION
54

PARTY
Republican

FIRST LADY
Laura Welch

CHILDREN
Barbara, Jenna

A long war
US soldiers remained in Iraq during Bush's presidency. Bush feared that withdrawing troops would cause instability.

Barack Obama

As the first African-American president, Barack Obama showed the opportunities open to all Americans in the 21st century. He gave his nomination acceptance speech on August 28, 2008, the 40th anniversary of Martin Luther King Jr.'s "I have a dream" speech, in which the civil rights leader spoke of racial equality. Born in Hawaii, Obama was the first president not born in the "lower 48" states. His father was from Kenya, and his mother was a white American from Wichita, Kansas. Obama served two terms.

Diagram of economic relationships

Organizing the community

After graduating from Columbia University in 1983, Obama moved to Chicago. He became a community organizer in a public housing development. He faced many challenges in his efforts to help the low-income residents he represented. The experience prepared him for work as a civil rights lawyer and a US senator.

An unusual childhood

Obama's parents divorced, and young Barack was raised by his mother and grandparents in Hawaii and Indonesia.

Rivalry within the party

Barack Obama and Hillary Clinton were neck-and-neck in the 2008 Democratic primaries. Clinton lost by a narrow margin and went on to support Obama's candidacy. She later became secretary of state in his cabinet.

Literary legacy

Obama wrote a memoir called *Dreams from My Father* and a political book called *The Audacity of Hope*, which became a best seller.

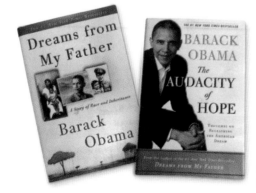

Obamamania

In 2004, Obama delivered the keynote address at the Democratic National Convention and became a political superstar. Young and eloquent, he appealed to a new generation of voters. His image was featured on magazines, billboards, and T-shirts. A biracial candidate who wasn't afraid to talk about race, Obama broke barriers.

Vice President Biden

Obama's vice president, Joe Biden, was elected to the Senate in 1972, at age 29. He brought a wealth of experience to the ticket in foreign affairs, drug policy, and national security.

"Yes We Can"

As a candidate with a message of hope and change, Obama used the slogan "Yes We Can" in his 2008 presidential run. His 2012 message was "Forward 2012."

The Affordable Care Act

In his first term, Obama signed into law his health-care reform plan, the Affordable Care Act—dubbed "Obamacare." The plan was challenged by opponents, but upheld by the US Supreme Court.

The first family

Obama met his wife, Michelle, while working at a Chicago law firm. They married in 1992 and have two daughters, Malia and Sasha.

Barack Obama

44TH PRESIDENT
2009–2017

BORN
August 4, 1961
Honolulu, Hawaii

INAUGURATED AS PRESIDENT
First term: January 20, 2009
Second term: January 21, 2013

AGE AT INAUGURATION
47

PARTY
Democratic

FIRST LADY
Michelle Robinson

CHILDREN
Malia, Sasha

Donald Trump

Billionaire real-estate developer Donald Trump was an unlikely presidential candidate. He spent his career as a businessman, not a politician, before making a bid for the White House. Pledging to "Make America Great Again," he said he would bring back "safety, prosperity, and peace."

Real-estate mogul

Trump began his career at his father's company, The Trump Organization. The younger Trump expanded the business, developing properties throughout New York and worldwide. He also invested in hotels, casinos, and golf courses.

Trump's platform

Trump was vocal about immigration reform. He created controversy when he proposed building a wall along the US border with Mexico. He also advocated cutting taxes and taking an aggressive stance against radical Islamic terrorism. Here, he gives a thumbs-up to supporters.

Media personality

Trump hosted the reality TV show *The Apprentice*, in which he judged contestants on their business ideas. The winner became his apprentice. "You're fired!" was his favorite phrase. He received a star on the Hollywood Walk of Fame in 2007.

Trump's star on the Hollywood Walk of Fame

TRU
TEXT "TRUMP" t
St. Louis, Mis
MAKE AMERICA GR

The Trump family

Trump is seen here on NBC's *Today Show* with his wife, Melania, and four of his five children—(from left) Tiffany, Eric, Ivanka, and Donald Jr. Ivanka in particular was a skilled public speaker and talked to voters about Trump's qualities as a father and a leader.

Tiffany, Trump's daughter from his second marriage

Melania supported her husband at campaign events

Vice President Pence

Michael "Mike" Pence was a member of the US House of Representatives, serving as Republican conference chairman. In 2012, he became governor of Indiana. He describes himself as a "Christian, conservative, and a Republican" and is known for his fiscal conservatism.

Donald Trump

45TH PRESIDENT
2017–

BORN
June 14, 1946
Queens, New York

INAUGURATED AS PRESIDENT
January 20, 2017

AGE AT INAUGURATION
70

PARTY
Republican

FIRST LADY
Melania Trump

CHILDREN
Donald Jr.
Ivanka
Eric
Tiffany
Barron

Winning the Republican nomination

Trump accepted the nomination in Cleveland, Ohio, on July 21, 2016. He secured the win after a hard-fought contest. Early in the election season, the field of candidates was large, with as many as 17 Republican hopefuls taking part in the primary debates.

Presidential Speeches

Presidents have always given speeches to calm the public's fears, inspire citizens to action, and account for their decisions. Some of these speeches have stood the test of time. The following excerpts from presidential speeches show how words can make a difference.

GEORGE WASHINGTON

George Washington's Farewell Address, published in newspapers on September 19, 1796, was an open letter to the public. He told citizens that he would not seek a third term. Above all, the much-loved first president cautioned Americans to work to preserve their hard-won independence.

. . . The unity of government which constitutes you one people is also now dear to you. It is justly so, for it is a main pillar in the edifice of your real independence, the support of your tranquility at home, your

Washington delivering his Farewell Address to Congress

peace abroad; of your safety; of your prosperity; of that very liberty which you so highly prize. But as it is easy to foresee that, from different causes and from different quarters, much pains will be taken, many artifices employed to weaken in your minds the conviction of this truth; as this is the point in your political fortress against which the batteries of internal and external enemies will be most constantly and actively (though often covertly and insidiously) directed, it is of infinite moment that you should properly estimate the immense value of your national union to your collective and individual happiness . . .

ABRAHAM LINCOLN

Abraham Lincoln's Gettysburg Address, November 19, 1863

The world will little note nor long remember what we say here, but it can never forget what they did here. It is for us the living rather to be dedicated here to the unfinished work which they

Lincoln at Gettysburg Cemetery

Printed copy of address

who fought here have thus far so nobly advanced. It is rather for us to be here dedicated to the great task remaining before us—that from these honored dead we take increased devotion to that cause for which they gave the last full measure of devotion—that we here highly resolve that these dead shall not have died in vain, that this nation, under God, shall have a new birth of freedom, and that the government of the people, by the people, and for the people, shall not perish from the earth.

FRANKLIN D. ROOSEVELT

Franklin D. Roosevelt's First Inaugural Address, March 4, 1933

. . . This is preeminently the time to speak the truth. . . frankly and boldly. . . This great Nation will endure as it has endured, will revive and will prosper. So, first of all, let me assert my firm belief that the only thing we have to fear is fear itself—nameless, unreasoning, unjustified terror which paralyzes needed efforts to convert retreat into advance. In every dark hour of our national life a leadership of frankness and vigor has met with that understanding and support of the people themselves which is essential to victory. I am convinced that you will again give that support to leadership in these critical days.

Roosevelt with Herbert Hoover on the way to his first inauguration

JOHN F. KENNEDY

John F. Kennedy's Inaugural Address, January 20, 1961

. . . [The] revolutionary beliefs for which our forebears fought are still at issue around the globe—the belief that the rights of man come not from the generosity of the state, but from the hand of God.

We dare not forget today that we are the heirs of that first revolution. Let the word go forth from this time and place, to friend and foe alike, that the torch has been passed to a new generation of Americans—born in this century, tempered by war, disciplined by a hard and bitter peace, proud of our ancient heritage—and unwilling to witness or permit the slow undoing of those human rights to which this Nation has always been committed, and to which we are committed today at home and around the world. . .

In the long history of the world, only a few generations have been granted the role of defending freedom in its hour of maximum danger. I do not shrink from this responsibility—I welcome it. I do

JFK with Peace Corps volunteers

not believe that any of us would exchange places with any other people or any other generation. The energy, the faith, the devotion which we bring to this endeavor will light our country and all who serve it—and the glow from that fire can truly light the world.

And so, my fellow Americans: ask not what your country can do for you—ask what you can do for your country.

My fellow citizens of the world: ask not what America will do for you, but what together we can do for the freedom of man.

RONALD REAGAN

Ronald Reagan's Evil Empire Speech, March 8, 1983

. . . I urge you to speak out against those who would place the United States in a position of military and moral inferiority . . . I urge you to beware the temptation of pride—the temptation to blithely declare yourselves above it all and label both sides equally at fault, to ignore the facts of history and the aggressive impulses of an evil empire, to simply call the arms race a giant misunderstanding and . . . remove yourself from the struggle between right and wrong and good and evil . . .

. . . [T]he struggle now going on for the world will never be decided by bombs or rockets, by armies or military might. The real crisis we face today is a spiritual one; at root, it is a test of moral will and faith . . .

I believe we shall rise to the challenge. I believe that communism

is another sad, bizarre chapter in human history whose last pages even now are being written. I believe this because the source of our strength in the quest for human freedom is not material, but spiritual. And because it knows no limitation, it must terrify and ultimately triumph over those who would enslave their fellow man.

Reagan at the podium

PRESIDENTIAL FIRSTS

- John Quincy Adams was the first president to be photographed.

- Andrew Jackson was the first president to survive an assassination attempt.

- Martin Van Buren was the first president born in the United States.

- John Tyler was the first vice president to rise to the presidency upon the death of a president.

- Grover Cleveland was the first president to have a child born in the White House during his time in office.

- William McKinley was the first president to ride in an automobile.

- Theodore Roosevelt was the first American to win the Nobel Peace Prize.

- Harry Truman was the first president to give a speech on television.

- Lyndon B. Johnson was the first president to name an African-American to his cabinet.

- Barack Obama was the first African-American president.

BOOKS BY PRESIDENTS

- *Personal Memoirs*, by Ulysses S. Grant, relates Grant's experiences in the Civil War.

- *The Rough Riders*, by Theodore Roosevelt, is based on his diary kept during the Spanish-American War.

- *Crusade in Europe*, by Dwight Eisenhower, is the story of World War II through his eyes.

- John F. Kennedy's *Profiles in Courage* highlights the work of great US senators.

- Jimmy Carter's *An Hour before Daylight* tells the story of his childhood.

- Bill Clinton's *My Life* is a portrait of a leader who decided early on to devote his life to public service.

Did you know?

FASCINATING FACTS

★ George Washington was the only president who never lived in the White House.

White House under construction

★ John Adams and Thomas Jefferson both died on the 50th anniversary of the Declaration of Independence. Not knowing that Jefferson had died, Adams's last words were "Jefferson lives."

★ Thomas Jefferson wrote his own epitaph. It did not mention his time as president.

★ Martin Van Buren, from Kinderhook, New York, was called "Old Kinderhook." The term O.K. gained popularity due in part to Van Buren's nickname.

★ James K. Polk fulfilled his campaign promises. He acquired California from Mexico, settled the Oregon dispute, set up a sub-treasury, and retired after one term.

★ Zachary Taylor did not vote until age 62. As a soldier, he did not have an official residence until then.

★ Franklin Pierce gave his 3,319-word inaugural address from memory.

★ James Buchanan was the only president who never married.

★ Chester A. Arthur was called "Elegant Arthur" because of his fashion sense.

Cartoon of Chester A. Arthur

★ Grover Cleveland was the only president elected to non-consecutive terms.

★ William H. Taft was the only president to serve as chief justice of the Supreme Court.

★ Dwight D. Eisenhower served in both World War I and World War II.

★ On July 21, 1969, Richard M. Nixon talked to the first astronauts on the moon by radio-telephone.

★ Richard M. Nixon is the only president to have resigned.

QUESTIONS AND ANSWERS

Q Who was the youngest person to be elected president?

A At age 43, John F. Kennedy was the youngest person elected president. Sadly, he was also the youngest to die in office, at age 46.

Franklin D. Roosevelt

Q How many presidents have been assassinated in office?

A Four. Lincoln was assassinated by John Wilkes Booth on April 14, 1865. Garfield was shot by an angry citizen and died on September 19, 1881. McKinley was killed by an anarchist in September 1901. Kennedy was shot by Lee Harvey Oswald on November 22, 1963.

Q Which president served the longest?

A Franklin D. Roosevelt served three terms and died in his fourth term. The Twenty-second Amendment now limits presidents to two terms.

Q What is the Secret Service?

A The United States Secret Service is a federal agency that protects the president, vice president, and their families.

Q Which presidents are pictured on US currency?

A Abraham Lincoln (penny and $5 bill), Thomas Jefferson (nickel and

$100,000 bill

$2 bill), Franklin D. Roosevelt (dime), George Washington (quarter and $1 bill), John F. Kennedy (half dollar), Andrew Jackson ($20 bill), and Ulysses S. Grant ($50 bill). William McKinley ($500 bill), Grover Cleveland ($1,000 bill), James Madison ($5,000 bill), and Woodrow Wilson ($100,000 bill) were featured on bills that have been discontinued.

Find out more

Washington, D.C., has been home to every chief executive since John Adams. A trip there is a great way to learn about the presidents. The National Mall runs from the Capitol to the Lincoln Memorial. The Washington Monument, a 555 ft (169 m) obelisk, is on the Mall. From the top, visitors can see more than 30 miles (48 km) to Washington's Mount Vernon home.

USEFUL WEBSITES

- For facts on White House history, visit The White House Historical Association: www.whitehousehistory.org
- For information on all the presidents, go to the source: www.whitehouse.gov
- For profiles of US presidents, go to: www.smithsonianeducation.org/students/idealabs/mr_president.html
- This University of Virginia site provides information on the presidents: millercenter.org/academic/americanpresident
- The Smithsonian's National Portrait Gallery contains presidential portraits: www.npg.si.edu
- The National Archives contains information on the presidential libraries: www.archives.gov/presidential-libraries

The White House
A tour of the White House gives a sense of the daily lives of the presidents, since each president made changes to the interior upon entering office. Tours are available to groups of 10 or more and must be scheduled through your Member of Congress. The White House Visitor Center offers fascinating exhibits relating to the executive mansion.

PLACES TO VISIT

MONTICELLO, CHARLOTTESVILLE, VA
Visitors to Thomas Jefferson's estate can tour the mansion, slave quarters, and grounds.

NATIONAL MUSEUM OF AMERICAN HISTORY, WASHINGTON, D.C.
The Smithsonian Institution's National Museum of American History preserves more than three million artifacts, including presidential items.

RONALD REAGAN PRESIDENTIAL LIBRARY, SIMI VALLEY, CALIFORNIA
The library features a re-creation of the Oval Office.

LYNDON B. JOHNSON HISTORICAL PARK, JOHNSON CITY, TEXAS
Visitors can see Lyndon Johnson's boyhood home and the LBJ Ranch.

ADAMS NATIONAL HISTORICAL PARK, QUINCY, MASSACHUSETS
The home of John Adams contains 11 historic buildings, which are set on 14 acres of land.

FORD'S THEATER, WASHINGTON, D.C.
A Lincoln Museum contains artifacts relating to the assassination.

HARRY S. TRUMAN NATIONAL HISTORIC SITE, INDEPENDENCE, MISSOURI
The white Victorian-style house was built by Bess Truman's grandfather. It was called the "Summer White House" when her husband was in office.

JOHN F. KENNEDY PRESIDENTIAL LIBRARY, BOSTON, MASSACHUSETTS
The library includes multimedia exhibits from events in JFK's life.

MOUNT RUSHMORE, KEYSTONE, SOUTH DAKOTA
The granite heads of George Washington, Thomas Jefferson, Theodore Roosevelt, and Abraham Lincoln at this historic site are each 60ft (18m) high. They were designed by sculptor Gutzon Borglum.

Mount Rushmore

Index

Acknowledgments

DK Publishing would like to thank:
The staff of the Smithsonian Institution, Washington, D.C., particularly Beverly Cox at the National Portrait Gallery, Larry Bird and Lisa Kathleen Graddy at the National Museum of American History, and Ellen Nanney, Linda Sheriff, and Kealy Gordon at Product Development and Licensing. Jaye Tang for design help. Alan Reason for additional illustrations. Tina Chambers, Lynton Gardiner, Dave King, and Matthew Ward for additional photography. Chris Bernstein for the index. Victoria Pyke for proofreading the relaunch version, and Vicky Richards and Antara Raghavan for editorial assistance on it.

PICTURE CREDITS:
(t: top, b: bottom, l: left, r: right, c: center, a: above)

Alamy Stock Photo: Evan El-Amin 61cr; **American Document Company:** 5t, 11, 14tl, 24cl, 25cl, 27tc; **Architect of the Capitol:** 68cl; **Associated Press AP:** 61bl;

Bettmann/Corbis: 69tr, 69bc; **Bridgeman Art Library:** 6tr, 24b, 27c; /Private Collection/Peter Newark American Pictures: 70bl; **Camera Press:** 50tr; /John Spaull: 71br; /Kellie Walsh/4eyesphotography.com: 64bl, 65cl (book cover from Profiles in Courage by John F. Kennedy. Copyright © 1955, 1956, 1961 by John F. Kennedy. Copyright renewed © 1983, 1984, 1989 by Jacqueline Kennedy Onassis. Foreword copyright © 1964 by Robert F. Kennedy. Reprinted by permission of HarperCollins Publishers); /Wilberforce House, Hull City Museum: 22tl; **Dreamstime.com:** Americanspirit 65clb, R. Gino Santa Maria / Shutterfree, Llc 66–67; **ET Archive:** 5b, 21cl, 30b; **Mary Evans Picture Library:** 6bl, 9tr, 12cla, bl, 17tl, 31br, 33br, 48tr; **J. Emilio Flores/Corbis:** 65cr; **Getty Images:** Brooks Kraft 67crb, Daniel Acker / Bloomberg 67ca, M. Tran / FilmMagic 66bl, Paul J. Richards / AFP 65cr, Pete Souza / The White House 65bc, Richard Cummins 66cl, Spencer Platt 67tl; **Andrew Gombert/epa/Corbis:**

64–5b; **Sonya Hebert/Dallas Morning News/Corbis:** 65bc; **Hulton Getty Images:** 44bl, c; **iStockphoto.com:** hept27 61tr; **Jupiter Images:** 71cla; /Abbie Rowe, National Park Service: 69tc; **Jeff Kowalsky/epa/Corbis:** 64tr; **Brooks Kraft/Corbis:** 62br; **Library of Congress:** 68tr, c, br; **Metropolitan Museum of Art, New York, U.S.A./ Bridgeman Art Library:** 4c; **Museum of American Political Life:** 62cl; **NASA:** 53t; **Peter Newark's Pictures:** 6br, 7tl, tc, 10bl, 12–13, 14c, 15tr, 18b, 22tr, cla, br, 23tr, bl, 32cr, 33tl, 35cl, 35br, 37bl, 38bl, bc, br, 40c, 42–3b, 44–5c, 45b, cr, 49tr, 50tl, 51cr, 53cl, 56cl; **Courtesy Obama for America:** 64cr; **Obama For America/Handout/Reuters/Corbis:** 64cl; **Popperfoto:** 8–9b, 49tl, b, 50–lb, 54br, 60bl, 61tl; **Reuters/Corbis:** 63tl, cr; **Smithsonian Institution:** 4tr, 6tl, 7bl, 8cl, bl, 9br, 10br, 12tl, tr, 13tr, 14br, 15br, 16cl, 17tr, 18tr, trb, 19tl, br, 23c, 24tr, c, 27cb, cr, br, 28tl, 29tc, ca, cb, 30tl, 31ca, 32t, 33bc, 35tr, bl, 36br, 37br, 38tr, 39tc, crb, 40bc, 41tc, tr, br, 46cl, cra, cr, crb, b, 48tl, er, 49tc, 52tl, cla, clb, 53c, 54tr, 55tc, ca, cb, 56tl, 58ca, cb, 60c, crb, 61trb, c, cb, 62tr, bl, 70tl; **Becker Collection:** 17br; /Corbis: 70crb; /Langbourn Washburn: 46t; /Library of Congress: 5cra; /Robert

G Myers: 37cl; /National Museum of American History: 4tl, 5crb, 7cr, 9tl, 10tl, 12clb, 16tc, tr, 17bl, 19bc, 20tl, 22bl, 28br, 30tr, 32br, 34tla, tlb, tr, 35c, 37tl, 45cl, cra, ca, 50bc, br, 53crb; /National Portrait Gallery: 4–5, 6c, 7cl, br, 8t, 10tr, 14tr, 15tl, c, bl, 16tl, br, 18tl, 19c, bl, 20tr, 20–21b, 21tr, 22cr, 23cl, cr, br, 25bl, 26cl, bl, 26–7b, 27tr, 28tr, cl, b, 29tl, tr, br, bl, 30cl, bl, 31cb, 32bl, 33tr, cl, 34b, 36tl, c, 37tr, c, cr, 38tl, cl, 39cl, 44bl, 45tr, 47bl, 51br, 52c, b, 54cl, 55br, 56bl, 58tl; **Dorothy Garfein:** 40tr; /Charles H. Phillips: 4bl; /Rosalind Solomon: 57br; /George D. Tames: 48, b; /Diana Walter: 58–59lb, 60l; **Science & Society Picture Library:** 30cr; **Stapleton Collection/Corbis:** 70tr; **Steven Starr/Corbis:** 65tc; **Tanen Maury/epa/Corbis:** 65tl; **Topham Picturepoint:** 1, 14bl, 25t, 39b, 40–lb, 41cr, 42tl, 43cr, 44cr, 47tl, tr, 51t, 53b, 55cl, bl, 56cr, br, 56–7b, 57tr, c, 58tr, 59c, 60tr, 61tr; **Valdrin Xhemaj/epa/Corbis:** 63b; **The White House:** 62tl.

All other images © Dorling Kindersley

For further information see:
www.dkimages.com